MW00768488

V:
A Mother's Victory

A Mother's Victory

V:
A Mother's Victory

Robin Morgan Roberson Potts

VANTAGE PRESS
New York

Published by Vantage Press, Inc.
516 West 34th Street, New York, New York 10001

Manufactured in the United States of America
ISBN: 0-533-12896-X

Library of Congress Catalog Card No.: 98-90732

0 9 8 7 6 5 4 3 2 1

This Journal Is Dedicated
to My Dream Team
Who Lived It

Zoph—He never wavered. He knew I would be well.

Ryle—Her compassion and can-do were limitless—entertainment to eyelash shopping.

Charles and Christie—their warm company at the cottage, rocking with Zoph on the porch while I slept off chemo.

Reed—sharing his steady stream of friends and daily basketball record-breaking dunks.

Morgan—my personalized music and comedy programmer and laugh-maker.

Frances and Bill Roberson—celebrating every step as a victory.

Katherine Potts—"I lifted you up to the Lord. I have prayed continuously."

Olivia and Riley Roberson—constant care plus milkshakes during chemo and assurance that I didn't look funny.

Dear Reader,

Do you have a husband, wife, son, daughter, or friend facing chemotherapy?

Your good health gives us strength . . . Ryle (daughter, 25) plays Annelle in *Steel Magnolias*—rich, witty lines—love it! Charles (son, 22) rescues with the Coast Guard. Reed (son, 17) is studying at Virginia Episcopal School—and practicing to be on the basketball team; slam-dunking. Morgan (son, 16) aggressively presses on every soccer game. His leadership is recognized.

Your work and your interests give us energy. All that you are and all that you do give us courage. My husband, Zoph, asks me, do I think of myself as sick. . . . He doesn't.

Chemo is harder on you than us. You suffer watching. Meals friends bring feed our spirit. Notes from friends are saved for the end of the day to share with my husband—a happy hour.

Are you facing chemo?

We'll celebrate that there is something out there to help us. We focus on what we can do—delegate the rest. We let our friends and family help us (we would help them). We keep our spirits up: this is our job, and it is a job. We tell ourselves night and day that there is nothing that somebody hasn't lived through. I did—nine years ago.

Yours, Robin
July 1995

Dear Reader,

When my mother, Robin Potts, was diagnosed with breast cancer, I really was not aware of the seriousness of her illness.

I can still vividly remember the day she told me she had breast cancer. I had just come in from soccer practice and my mother was busy clanking pots in the kitchen, which was my mother's everyday ritual. Right when I saw her, I could tell she wanted to tell me something. And I was right because she asked me to follow her to the foyer where she calmly had a seat. She began by reminding me about the doctor's appointments she had been going to and the tests she had been given, but I'm not one for details so I, sweating and half out of breath from soccer practice, told her to get to the point. She then calmly came right out and said, "Morgan, I have breast cancer," and continued by saying, "We're going to beat this."

Beat what? I was thinking. I did not understand the seriousness of breast cancer. I was a young adolescent. I figured you could pop a couple pills and the problem would be solved. After all, that's what I did when I was sick, take some pills and my earache or headache was gone. I did not realize she would have to go through radiation and chemotherapy, which, at that time, made you horribly sick because there weren't any pills that could eliminate the nausea caused by the treatment. And treatments were not even a sure thing. So here I was after my mother had told me the awful news, just standing there clueless about what really was going on. I didn't know what to do or how to react. So my mother stood up, gave me a hug, and told me she loved me.

During the treatments, things started to get really strange to me. First, she had radiation treatment. Of course, I didn't have a clue what this was, but I kept my mind busy by trying to imagine what it was. Maybe they exposed my mother to an atomic bomb blast or just zapped her full of X rays. Hell, I thought if you are exposed to radiation, it would cause people to have a third eye, something freakish like that. Well, anyway, from what I could gather at the time, the radiation treatment didn't work, so they had to move on to what is called chemotherapy and that is when things started to get a little out of the ordinary at the Potts house.

My mother no longer cooked for us; instead friends and neighbors had us over for dinner or brought us home-cooked meals to our own house. And boy, did I love that. I'm not saying my mother is a bad cook or anything; it was just a pleasant change from eating fish sticks and Spaghet-tios everyday.

My mother had quite a few treatments or cycles of chemo, and every time she came home from the hospital af-ter receiving treatment, she would get severely ill. She would vomit and gag and cough almost constantly. My room was right beside her bedroom at the time, and all I heard were her footsteps running to the bathroom, the flick of the light switches, and the sound of my mother's gagging in the toilet. Those noises terrified me, and it happened many nights during her chemo. I could not figure out why in the world my mother was so sick. After all, she went to the hospital to get treatment for being sick in the first place and now she had to go through this too. I think at one point I actually believed she was exposed to someone else's germs at the hospital; after all, that's where a lot of sick people were and always got sick as a dog. What did I know? I was just a little kid.

Shortly into the chemotherapy, after one of my mom's nausea spells had subsided, she called me into her bathroom where she was standing facing the mirror right above the bathroom lavatory. Her hair looked a little unusually nappy. I mean it was nappy before because she had been in bed for days, but it looked a little worse. I then glanced in the sink and saw little clumps of hair. I didn't know if she was giving herself a trim and wanted help with the back or what. Then my mom said one word, "Look." Right as she said that, she reached to her head and pulled gently on several strands of hair; and they came right out. Her hair was falling out!!

She continued to pull out hair as I stood there with my eyes wide open and my chin on the floor. She began to laugh as she would alternate hands. I snapped out of my zone and asked her, "What did you do, drink a gallon of sour milk?" She laughed and then explained to me it is what happens when you undergo chemotherapy. And as she explained it to me, I began to pull at her hair also. It would come right out. It was kind of like pulling off a big chunk of cotton candy that you buy at the fair. That's how easy her hair was coming out. So not only did the chemo make her sick, it also made her lose her hair. And to me at this time, chemo did not seem like a very good treatment. I mean, my mom was falling apart, for crying out loud.

The next morning my mother was wearing a bandana, scarf, or turban of some sort on her head. Her hair had completely fallen out. My brother Reed and I were sitting at the kitchen table, eating our usual Pop Tarts for breakfast when we saw our mom's new headdress. She told us she was completely bald and asked if we wanted to see. I immediately said yes as she ripped off the cloth covering her head. She stuck out her tongue and began waving her head back and forth and laughing. Reed did not want any part of it; he had seen enough, as he quickly did an about-face. Her bald head kind of freaked him out. Me, I just thought she looked like the Black bald guy on Sesame Street.

My mom ended up getting two wigs to wear while she was sporting the Kojak look, and her favorite thing to do was wait 'til everyone was comfortable, walk into a room, and rip off her wig and shake her slick cranium around the room. Reed would always be the first to turn his head; it gave him nightmares, I think. I even got her to do it for some of my friends. And after my mom would leave the room, my friends would lean to me and say, "Your mom is nuts!!!"

My mother would eventually beat the demon called breast cancer. Now that I look back, I don't see how she did it, how she kept her composure, how she kept her sense of humor, how she kept on being a mom while she was going through this enormous ordeal. I didn't realize until later how serious her condition really was, and I'm kind of glad it happened back then when I couldn't grasp it because I don't know how I would have handled it if it were happening today.

I think there is something positive that our family has learned, especially my mother from the whole ordeal. And that is to enjoy life while you're here and take advantage of every opportunity that comes before you.

—Morgan

Reed's Recollections

My mother's illness was probably the most difficult thing I have had to deal with so far in my life. I remember being up at prep school talking with my father and his telling me that Mom would be having surgery in the morning (spring 1988). I had no idea at the time of the seriousness of what was going on. It wasn't until I got home for the summer that I realized how sick my mother was. The following year would be a tough one, especially for Mom who would have to endure countless radiation treatments, sickness, and fatigue. I can remember sleeping at night and hearing Mom in the bathroom getting sick, as well as all of her hair falling out, both of which were side effects of the radiation treatment. Looking back on this, the thing that probably helped Mom beat cancer more than anything was her spirit. While she was going through this, she remained positive and resilient and just knew she was going to beat this thing and she did.

May 26, 1997
Reed

Recollections of Charles

When I found out Mom had breast cancer, I was in the Coast Guard stationed in Coinjock, North Carolina. Dad had called me and told me that Mom was in the hospital and had or was going to have her breast removed before or after, I can't remember. I immediately asked for leave and started a long 2-1/2 hour drive home. At the time, I really didn't know anything about cancer except that it was real bad. Some of my thoughts were: *Why my mom? Why not somebody else? How bad was it? Was she going to make it through?* I kept going back to one thought: *What if she didn't make it? What would our family be like without her?* I could never picture what it would be like. When I got to the hospital, Dad and Mom were in the room. When I saw her smile, it was very reassuring. I missed a lot of my mom's battle with cancer with me being stationed out of town. I would see bits and pieces of it when I came to visit. The one thing that was always the same on each visit was my mom's will to beat it, and she did.

Charles Potts
June 1997

Reflections from Ryle

I wanted her to feel with me . . . as she always had. That I would be there . . . whenever and wherever I would be there. We both knew it was there . . . she felt it, experienced it, lived it. I didn't talk to it, I talked to her, I wasn't there for it, I was there for her. It did not need me to be there for it. It had my acknowledgment and the respect for the time and space it needed.

There is no doubt in my mind why she emerged victorious. She believed in the life force that has always sustained her and continues to sustain her. We survived and emerged as a direct result of her surviving and emerging. She gave us the emotional and psychological strength to cure our own various incapacitating ills.

My personal one was the "fear of the unknown." Knowing her and loving her has taught me that fearing the unknown is fearing life and that fearing life is not living.

Thank you, Mother, for teaching me to live.

I love you.

Ryle
May 2, 1997

Zoph's Recollections

I felt total devastation from Robin's encounter with cancer. I had always repressed the idea that anyone in my family could be confronted with cancer. I was particularly appalled with the prospect of breast cancer for women. It happened to other unfortunate souls. I couldn't imagine anyone having parts of their body removed. Poor souls, but it was someone else, not my concern.

I first felt the mass in Robin's breast and I knew immediately that we had a problem. Why Robin? Why my wife, someone so special?

The living of years had prepared me for most anything, but not for this. How could I appear to be calm and reassuring in the face of such a devastating reality?

Through chemotherapy, loss of hair, and physical devastation, Robin's will prevailed. She gave us all hope and strength. There was never a question that she would overcome the unbelievable that attacked her.

Robin led the charge. She was positive, proactive, and her normal, lovely self. No way was a bout with cancer going to bring her down. I will never forget her spirit and her determination to overcome her illness.

Robin lost her hair, but no problem. She had the most attractive wig anyone could imagine. She never felt sorry for herself. She really felt that she had a mission to help others with their problems.

Let me say that throughout the process I learned a great deal about the strength of the human spirit to overcome and prevail in the face of overwhelming odds. There is always hope. Robin never gave up. She decided to fight very hard and accept the medical help that was offered. She has won her battle. Positive attitude and just plain hard work pay off. Don't ever give up.

Zoph
May 2, 1997

Deepest Gratitude

Hannah and James Bagwell—"I knew you needed something to wear." Dresses that would fit over the tubes and bandages. Myrtle Patterson—"I'll sit right here with you. You can sleep. I'll watch the door." Gayle and Bill Morgan—a visit sitting on my hospital bed. Freddie and Puddin' Potts—rocking on the cottage porch. Kay Potts Andrew—"You'll have an uphill fight, but you'll make it!" Mary Ann Potts Toller—home for Noel, a unique treat. Bet and Tom Archie—"Make me a list of twenty friends for your birthday lunch . . . thirty-five? Fine!" Marcia Dunn—"Tell Bill and Frances that they are your team and you need them now." (Bill and Frances were in Italy. How to tell them?). Linda Kinsey—"Your counts are too low to get chemo? That's good! That means it's working!" Terri and Ray Bergevin—"We wanted to do something to get your counts up"—dinner. Bill and Jean Weatherspoon—"Come for the weekend!" Pat and Sue Brown—Raleigh—river strawberry daiquiris. Dr. Mary Raab, "What we want is a cure, so take the strongest medicine there is." Nurse Geneva Everett—"How's that paper coming?" Dr. Phil Coleman—"Call Zoph, we need to talk." Dr. Barr Coleman—"No, you don't have to look." Pack Hindsley—a camellia on my hospital pillow. Jan Hindsley and Pat Hill—suppers and strawberry picking. Kack and Henry

Hodges and Katherine Hodges Hall—even at the hospital, cheer, from day one. Edna Woolard and Diane Woolard Smith—"We'll make you a bosom." Mary Asby—calling. Josephine Winters—bringing smiles and cuisine in the A.M. looking like *Town and Country.* Nancy Carpenter—on my steps with homemade spaghetti: "I just wanted to help." Jane Griffin—pop visits. Energy! Jane Wilson—pep talks. Mildred Rumley—joke book. Professors Marguerite Perry and Grace Ellenberg—calls: "We just heard. This is terrible. We love you." Jerry Bron—confident to all of us. I.B. and Josephine Paul—prayers and visits. Constance Pierce—"Combine your real life and your cancer journal. . . . I wrote a book in your cottage this winter." Marsha Hackney and Beth—"What can we do for you? Anything . . . of course we can find an anniversary card for your parents!" Hodges Hackney—For the first time, my wig was just off, and a little peach fuzz of hair and Hodges sees me: "You look beautiful." Dee Harrington—perfume to the hospital. Delores and Carlos Harris (Chelsea screaming in the car)—friendship and green peas. Mary Bilbro, Claire Darrow, Peggy Lewis, Evelyn Smith, Lisa Walker, Alida Sawyer, Jean Lee—home cooking: together time. Juliette and Bob McDonough—special visits and creations. Erin Tayloe—letter sharing Broadway. Diane Gerard—Robin to Olivia: "Diane's given up on me—she's sent me a prayer book!" Olivia: "No. She hasn't given up on you." Marshall Tayloe—"We've gone over and over your mammogram. There is no sign of anything. We are so sorry. So sorry for what you're going to have to go through." Jennifer Kummer—"Aren't you glad you didn't have cancer in the 60's?" Bubbles Seighman—balloons and company in the hospital. Pauline Worthy—letter: "I wished you lived next door. I would be right over." Sue Loy and Brick Pemberton—"We had this thirty years ago." Taylor Whichard—"Here are some strawberries for you, Mrs.

Potts. I hope you feel better." Kindergartners, first and second graders—my French students: "I hope the hole beside your hearts gets better." Robert Belcher—my principal, in 1987: "Can Channel 7 TV come into your French class?" Mary Hazel and John Lucas—"We want to help you anyway we can. Just let us know. . . . Of course we can take you to the doctor today. . . . Can we take you to chemo too?" Professor Bertie Fearing—"This is the perfect time for you to work." Professor Luke Whisnant—"Of course you can have an extension. Take care. Keep in touch." Sandra Buckman—how to focus book: a watershed. Faye Corey—special card. Mae Ray—books Mother and I would enjoy together. Sarah Stilley Thompson—constant cards. Jo Lewis—visit. Nell and Milo Gibbs—surprises. Sam Long—travel letters. Wooly Modlin—in touch after thirty years. Pat Jefferson Gautier—notes from a hero since sixth grade. Alice McLure—the unexpected angle: laughs. Anne Grist; "I just want to help." (As she brings in home cooking). Ophelia Dixon: "I remember when my daughter went through this. I really want to help you." Jane and Sally McCotter—flowers and birds. Pat Robbins—kindnesses. Kay, Cameron Scott, and Sarah Katherine Buckman—picking fresh berries and bringing supper to the cottage. Rachel and Ashley Futrell—energy. Hank and Fran Stevenson and Bill and Jane Page—an immediate view of flowers at the hospital. Gale Champion—lunch and laughs. Margaret Brubaker—specialized shopping and camaraderie. . . . Many kind souls boosted my team and me: The memories are crystal.

Yours,
Robin

V:
A Mother's Victory

April 1, 1997

In 1988 I was bionic, jogging three miles daily, popping out of trash cans at the elementary schools as French Oscar, singing on Saturday in a gorilla suit, performing "La Marseillaise" at malls.

My flight to Las Vegas with my husband in the spring of '88 was business and pleasure, the latest of many elegant trips. At forty-five, when friends mentioned getting everything fixed, I would laugh, but wonder if I should (but, how could I with no nerve? End of consideration of beauty enhancement surgery).

My husband had thought that breast cancer was one of the two worst things that could happen. He's forgotten the other. He says that before 1988, he would never read anything about breast cancer because it was too awful to think about.

It's 1999 and we love life and people and each other. I'm still bionic, other people say, but I never was really. I do know fear of leaving the planet and what works to combat it—focus and resources. Who I used to be can't compare with this new (chastened) gal. I wish those of you who want to help someone you love cope could know that you can—here's proof. It's teamwork—a first for me (a former wanna-be self-starter/sustainer). I believe now that my trauma of 1988 is still transforming me daily with more power and vision, but I know about giving up—and I know eternal gratitude that I did not have my way.

Robin

April 1988—When I am well, I will need these notes to jog my memory so that I can help someone else along as I have been.

April 5, 1988—Tuesday night, 9:15. I'm getting in the shower and notice my left bosom is huge. Zoph is reading. I go to the medical journal. There's no information on swollen bosoms. It's not one of the seven danger signs.

"Zoph, do I look funny?"

"No, why?"

"I've just got one big one. And it's not in the medical book. Are you sure I don't look funny?"

"No. I don't see any difference."

April 8, 1988—Charles's graduation in Yorktown, Virginia, from the Diesel Mechanic School of the U.S. Coast Guard. Christie Lewis goes with us. We tour Jamestown and lunch together. Zoph and I fly to Las Vegas for the U.S. Broadcasters' meeting.

April 9, 1988—Olivia's birthday. All four of us drive to Hoover Dam. Diahann Carroll's at 52 at Caesar's Palace. I decide to get big bosoms like that sometime. My one big bosom is still big.

Diahann Carroll and Vic Damone sing and talk on stage. He says, "Doesn't she look great?" The audience applauds as she enters—sequins, neckline to the waist, and hemline to the waist. "She has a trainer and works out every day." Carroll sings gutsy, like Garland. I decide to get bosoms like that someday.

April 10, 1988—Las Vegas. Sunday. Radio people. Concern for expanded AM band considerations. Speak up to the FCC about prospective applications. Going to happen!

People queuing in 8:15 A.M. Military band at 10:00 A.M. "Mine Eyes Have Seen the Glory." President Reagan arrives. We see on screens around the hall. Military marches: "God Bless the USA," "Off We Go Into the Wild Blue Yonder."

"Mr. Las Vegas," Wayne Newton: "I'm picked because I'm not ethnic or Indian."

Applause for the Air Force Orchestra. Audience rises for the colors. A man on the end of our aisle doesn't. Young soldiers bring five flags.

Wayne Newton: "I'm a little awkward, like Elizabeth Taylor's next husband."

Chairman of the NAB—golf joke (Eddie Fritz); "The President and Mrs. Reagan!" Everybody stands. That same man doesn't. "Today we're honoring one of our own. He, sportscaster. Des Moines. He's reached out for broadcasters. To the first president to work for the deregulation of the broadcasting industry. Committed to the free market."

President Reagan: "I know you at the entertainment mecca have one thing on your mind—foreign policy. As for me . . . association of town criers . . . oppose big governments . . . opposed Fairness Doctrine. Now could I enlist your help? I nominated Bradley Hall to the FCC last fall. Isn't it time the Senate took action? I've got legislation to propose. New legislation to limit commercials during my old movies. 1923. Warren Harding. First President by radio. Truth . . . when truth is far from our minds. So I want to address foreign policy. Arms reduction. Our fundamental approach. We have permitted our nuclear arms to dwindle during the detente in the '70s. My hope is that the Senate will ratify the IN treaty. In the '60s we slashed defense; '70s we were dealing from weakness. Today we deal from strength. Why, of course the Senate didn't agree in the '70s. They could get something for nothing. Some have called me a bullnosed warmonger. Now we know strength works. Hope for bipartisan support for strategic defense mechanisms. Expensive but an investment in world peace when you consider the alternatives. In our relations with the Soviets, let us always agree on human rights. We are helping Nicaragua and Afghanistan to stand by the freedom fighters. I'll be speaking about human rights in the near future—maybe to be announced in Geneva, a total withdrawal from Afghanistan. At Geneva Summit in '85, Gorbachev and I started exchanges—Horowitz, Gorbachev, Academics and Science. Next month in Moscow, I'll expand exchanges, people to people, technology. In West: breakthroughs. In Communist World: economic stagnation. Krhruschev said, 'We will bury you,' but the Soviet citizen spends two hours to shop for necessities daily.

"Consider *Forbes* cover story: Coming Computer Development. You ain't seen nothing yet. 10,000—fold more productivity. The end isn't in sight. Mend the physicist: 'We're not going to need the government to bail out technology.' Freedom unburdened. The Soviets must open or fall further behind. Oppression. Open to Western Media. All books. Mr. Gorbachev, open to Solzhenitzven. We have been divided too long. Let us build world anew. As Henry VIII said to each of his six wives: 'I won't keep you long.' "

"The Great Communicator Award to President Reagan—for your dedication to the First Amendment and belief in broadcasting. For a lifetime of achievement."

April 11, 1988—Las Vegas. Conferences. Monday. Advertising. GM's ten assumptions. Difference between management and leadership. Vision occurs when one is working on massive information and recognizes a good idea in others. We pass along "Dressing for Success," "Time Management," etc. for wisdom. What works: Self-knowledge, commitment, dedication, continued learning. Develop new

4

dollars. Grow market share. Fifty percent more magazines out than ten years ago. Seventy-eight percent in Houston don't take a newspaper. Teach. Train. Retrain. At IBM forty hours a year in training. Example: The employer who has a waiting list of people wanting to work with him because he spends so much on training. Plaques for employees who have completed training. Train all as though they are a life-long employee. Priority must be teaching. "If we don't change directions, we're likely to end up where we are headed."—a Chinese philosopher. It has to be a religious experience. We have to speak up before legislation. Commercials. Powerful words. Furniture Company in Kentucky: Those words were not put in his mouth. "I can put a picture on radio that I can't do on TV." The Nissan gal doubled my business. What do you care about getting newspapers mad—they don't help you anyway. Tell your sales staff they don't need to sell radio as part of a media mix. How far you go in life depends on

how tender you are with the young,
how tender you are with the ambitious,
how tender you are with the old,
how tolerant you are with the weak and strong, because
    someday in life you will have been all of these.

"Let's get away from facts and figures. Let me drop a bomb. Sound can inspire some strong thoughts. We can see only one-half the day. We can hear all the time. Hearing is linked to self-preservation. Hearing is survival. Gets inside the mind of your customer. Sound engages all other senses. Example: Bacon cooking. Juice pouring. Can take you up or down. Sound. Powerful. The first active sense—the first stimulus from the outside world. Sounds for Texas Gulf promo. Gulls—birds—water lapping—wind. Sound: Set the alarm to be on time. Time breaks through the clutter: conveys complex emotions; frustration; exhilaration; gets you feeling and thinking. United Airlines bought Gershwin's *Rhapsody in Blue.* Music can challenge your emotions. Example: *Chariots of Fire* theme. Music moves people, speaks to their hearts like nothing else. Martin Luther King from the Lincoln Memorial: That speech—Hilltops of N.H. heightened Alleghenies—from Mississippi . . . from every mountain. How powerful a skilled human voice can be. Reaching your customers with emotion. Radio can reach a gut level. Can catalyze your customer's feelings. Three tools of radio: Voice, music, sound; intrusive, demands attention. The best tools in combo. Incredibly powerful. Example: Tribute to the space shuttle tragedy. Time to celebrate this new adventure, fifteen seconds . . . teach a course (Christa McAuliffe's voice) in history and hope to return with a picture of what an ordinary person sees in space. Noise. Malfunction. "It is with deep sorrow this morning . . . (silence . . .). We will never forget them as we saw them this morning, as they prepared to touch the face of God."

April 11, 1988—Las Vegas. Conference. License renewal. Include more info if you know it's going to be asked for. The quickest way to lose your license: fudge . . . hedge. The commission's looking for overboard practices, of course (does not want to hear of fraudulent billing). If the man forgets something in logging—put it in with a note of explanation. You could lose your license for arrogant disregard of standards. The commissioner will consider a station's whole file (complaints). A lot is up to you. Relicensing. NAB has a renewal packet. They're looking:

1. At outside the station
2. At inspection files
3. Have an updated inspection file

4. Teach operations and monitor readings
5. Employer report
6. Ownership report

You're very vulnerable to misrepresentation. Programming: Issues of principle and community. Ten days after the end of each quarter you must put it on your public inspection file. Be part of significant issues. Moderator: J. Bowmann. W. Hargrove. M. Rosenberg. R. Stewart. The commissioner never said to deal with every issue. Where is your principal obligation? To your community of license. Even our AM is extremely involved. (You are at risk if you don't on PM be aggressive . . . with public service. Document it.) Petition to deny. Challenge. Completing application. Complaint from the public. Renewal time. Seven years. Expectancy based on serving community of license. Build your reservoir. Did the licensee act reasonably? (Advantage to living in the county—add to the discussion of issues in your community.) Example: Iowa. Not many issues. Sidewalks. The lake might stink but. . . . To specialize your issues toward your target audience. Can do. But the commission doesn't rank the importance of issues. That the station is an outlet for people to address issues. What if ninety percent of public service is at 4:30 A.M. Sunday? Equal employment? Difficult: new cases. Shift figures and data. FCC: two aspects. Don't discriminate method of recruitment of minority races. Even to meet the numerical standard is not good enough. Recruitment must be emphasized. Effective records: What sources you use and number of recruits. Periodically pick up records to use if you're getting enough applications. Possible paperwork mandated by FCC if standards aren't met. Job description and recruitment methods. Whether a station can rely on Washington, work force, numbers? The commission is not playing a numbers game.

The emphasis is on what steps are you taking to attract applicants to prevent payoffs (Green mail—a cottage industry—in exchange for not filing—or petitioning) to deny. Does the commission have any authority to stop this? The NAB is troubled about that. Hot issue. Troubling. June is the deadline when renewals start.

April 12, 1988. When we arrive home Tuesday, Zoph mentions what he has been keeping to himself. Zoph thinks I need a checkup. He doesn't want to alarm me, but he noticed a mass in my big breast in Las Vegas.

April 15, 1988—*Une visite de Maren (Allemande). L'invitée de la famille de Bill Zachman à l'Ecole Eastern.* I'm sitting in Ned's (Dr. Hill's) office for a checkup, trying to get back to teach school and welcome my special students.

Friday 9:30. Ned says he doesn't think it's anything to worry about. He sends me to Dr. Phil Coleman.

10:00. Ned (the G.P.) to Phil (the surgeon): "She has a fibrosis disease but . . . (I'm supposed to be hosting German students at Eastern at 10:30). Phil says he doesn't think it's anything to worry about—that maybe it's an inflammation: "Take Indocin for 10 days. Maybe it will dissolve." I miss the German students, but I'm teaching by 11:30.

Comment fait le temps en Allemagne maintenant? J'espère que vous reviendrez un jour en été. Peut-etre il y a une possibilité que vous voudrez retourner pour assister à une université? Quels sujets vous intéressent comme une profession?

April 27, 1988—Wednesday. Fran and Daddy are leaving Friday for Paris on the Concorde. Phil says the mass must come out. . . .

Tuesday May 3: "I don't think you have anything to worry about." My last ECU class is tonight. My professor knows that I'm strung out and probably won't show. I can't do my work knowing the possibilities.

May 3, 1988—Tuesday. Outpatient surgery. Nurse Hazel. I comment on her nice big bosoms. She says they're overrated. Hers are waist-hangers. Her sister-in-law wants her to put a Greek goddess statue in her garden. She says, "No. I don't want my husband to know where they're supposed to hang."

4:00 P.M. To Jerry Bron (our minister at First Presbyterian), (me): "I saw Ann Miller at the Club Saturday night. She says that Chris has charmed all his teachers again. She says she should have been a nun." Jerry: "We'll take her. A little soiled, but we'll take her!" I sleep for twenty-one hours afterwards—1:00 A.M.—10:00 P.M. Wed. Phil: "By and large, it looks benign."

May 4, 1988—Wednesday. Fran and Daddy are in Florence, Italy. At 3:00 I go to Phil's office. He sees Zoph's not with me and calls him. "The tumor had benign characteristics, but it was malignant. You need a radical mastectomy, and I have scheduled you for tomorrow."—"Me? Do you have the wrong room? The wrong person?"

"I've called Zoph. He's on his way. Do you want to go on over to the hospital and get a good night's sleep or come in the morning?" (Phil).

Ryle is at home. Olivia arrives. I tell her: "I can't cry. I've got to make it look like a piece of cake because it could happen to Ryle." Riley arrives. Olivia: "You can now. Go ahead and cry now."

Pat Robbins substitutes Tuesday—Friday.

Shock sets in. We arrive. I'm crying. Can't talk. See Hank going toward an elevator. I sit in the lobby as Zoph checks me in. A blossom from Paul and Marcia breaks the spell of terror. I get my breath and stop crying.

May 5, 1988—Thursday. The Mother's Day charms for Fran and Granny are being done by Tom Stewart. My surgery—Barr: "There're some bad looking lymph nodes. We'll know Monday." Called Gayle Morgan at 7:00 A.M. to send

9

cute things to the hospital . . . gowns. In the waiting room with Zoph: Olivia, Riley, Jerry Bron, Kay. Stopping by to check: Hannah, Linda Kinsey, Paul Dunn, Kack and Henry Hodges, and Gayle Morgan. Olivia nurses me. Pack Hindsley brings me a camellia.

May 6, 1988—Friday—Flowers and friends. Nook and Hannah guard the door so I can sleep. They don't let in lunch either. Olivia nurses. Olivia tends to all things big and small. Zoph and I walk the halls. A little girl down the hall will be in a brace for months.

Visiting: Marsha (at home), Jerry Bron, Martha Seighman (Bubbles), Linda Kinsey, Bill Morgan, Elizabeth Propst, Carol Jones, Pat and Sue Brown, Bet Archie, Joe Jenkins, George Miller.

May 7, 1988—Supper Club Dance—We were going to take Margaret and Doug Brewbaker as guests. I'm home from the hospital. I have two drains, tubes coming out of my chest attached to balloons, which I pump every six hours, put the drain in a measuring cup, and note it to show Phil Tuesday when he thinks he will remove one of them. At 7:00 Doug and Margaret, Marti and David Sparrow pop in, dressed and en route to the dance.

Flowers flood in.

May 8, 1988—Sunday. It's Mother's Day. Fran's in Rome. We take a picnic to Granny. She loves her Ryle, Reed, Morgan, Charles's medallion. Charles's captain gives him a free weekend because of me. We go to the cottage. Christie, Morgan, and Charles put the wind surfer together. Hannah gave me a pale pink dress, which the balloons fit under well.

May 9, 1988—Monday. Riley and Olivia drive to Raleigh to pick up Bill and Fran to tell them about me. Riley can't talk about it. Olivia does the talking. Marcia Dunn walks with me this afternoon. At 1:15 Phil tells us I need chemotherapy, in his opinion . . . that Dr. Raab in Greenville will review my case and make her strategy. Marcia advises to tell Bill and Fran that I need them—that they are my team. I was really frustrated—how to handle this so they would be hit the least—but that's not possible. So since I know how much they love me and want to help, the only thing to do is for all of us to pull together hard . . . and live fully.

Phil has been telling us, "I don't think you have anything to worry about" so much that when he says today that three lymphs out of twenty were malignant and then assigns me to Dr. Raab, I listen up for "You're going to be fine" or "Dr. Raab will fix you up." I feel stunned.

Mother and Daddy arrive at our house at 9:30 from Europe. They like the Berthiers, Chantal, and Beatrice. They look young—like Peace Corps people. They hug me and want to know everything. (Ken's birth; Andrew).

May 10, 1988—Jane Wilson had a mastectomy, chemo, and radiation last year. She's my river neighbor. She calls to help. We plan to go to Greenville for a wig. I woke up in terror at 5:00. Can't sleep. Immeasurable fear. Crying. Zoph, too. Lindsay Kinsey instructs Dorothy Taylor's granddaughter at Harper's to switch shoulder straps on a floozie dress for the beach festival.

May 11, 1988—Mary Wilson and Tillie bring supper. Walks to the airport daily—three miles. 5:00 A.M. Terror. Shaking fears. Zoph, too. Jane and I at the Friendly Wig Shop. Chic cut. Jane flashes a mental picture of Anna and Guy when she had difficult moments.

May 12, 1988—Thursday. Mother and Daddy are in shock about me. Their phone's ringing. They're trying to get their focus while rebounding from jet-lag. I slept until 6:30, so then I decided to flash a mental picture of Zoph, Ryle, Charles, Reed, and Morgan. That makes me cry and starts "the fear" again. Zoph and I laugh—I should have left well enough alone. Phil didn't give us anything to cling to . . . no

"You'll be fine"—nothing except "Dr. Raab is wonderful. So nice." Who cares how nice she is? I just want her to fix me up.

May 13, 1988—Phil takes out the second drain. We miss a party at Lee and Josephine Winters. We go to Morehead and to the WDLX-sponsored Beach Festival. Morgan and Latham go with us. Zoph thinks I look gorgeous in my silver one-strap dress. Riley and Olivia, too. Lee Ann Tankard marries today.

May 14, 1988—Saturday. We enjoy dinner out with Doug and Margaret Brubaker and Diane and Bubba Gerard with Miller Company wild people.

Jane Wilson: "I've never heard the words 'you will be cured.' Now maybe you will, but I never have. Once one technician in the radiology department said: 'Well, cancer's a good thing to have because you can get rid of it. Unlike heart disease!' "

Jane Wilson confirms: Doctors don't talk about ones getting well, but they cite case histories. I finally knew better than to expect Dr. Raab to say she would fix me right up.

May 15, 1988—Sunday. Glenda and Rick Potts, Diana and Richard Young, Liz and Russ Cooke, and Frank Sheldon host a brunch at the Civic Center. We're still at the beach. My mastectomy arm is very touchy. Phil said it would be for months. Riley swims in the cold ocean. Olivia and I walk the beach. Latham works out my Texas Gulf comparison mathematically—Texas Gulf is one-half the size of New York City (area).

May 16, 1988—Monday. I see Phil at 1:45. Bet Archie brings supper. It is wonderful to be able to sit down to supper together. I never realized what bringing the food in to the sick means. It's not just food; it's time spent together. I don't yet have the stamina to shop, much less haul in groceries. Ryle's my laundress. I undergo a CAT scan, a liver and bone X ray. All look normal.

May 17, 1988—Mary Bilbro cooks and coordinates supper. Her pod of teachers cook. Delores and Carlos Harris arrive at 9:00 with peas. A nice visit. (Chelsea's screaming in the car.)

May 18, 1988—Wednesday. Mary Asby is cooking and coordinating supper tonight. Zoph, Mother, and I go to see Dr. Raab at 10:30. At 12:30 she really sees us. She is super nice and positive. "What we want is a cure," she says. In a nutshell she says: Exams every 3 to 4 months after chemo. Stay as much to my normal routine as possible. Trips are fine during chemo. Keep on jogging. I may tire more easily. I will be able to do about seventy-five percent of what I was used to. Base line checks—halfway through and afterwards. Then once a year (mammogram, bone-scan, chest X ray). No connection to arm problem. Eat well-balanced diet. Variable effect on bone marrow. Blood count every week. Can get in Beaufort County. One hour for chemo. Weight should stay the same. Six chemo treatments 3 to 4 weeks apart. Then two months of rest. Then 3 to 4 more chemo. There is a possibility that the tumor was there for several years. On the second chemo, June 15, I will have the Muga—a heart check—to see if the chemo is damaging the heart. Eat lightly before chemo. BCH will call in lab results. I can call Marvene to answer any questions. She'll give me the chemo. (Linda Kinsey tells me that Marvene's mother had one mastectomy at twenty-one and the other at twenty-four, and she's seventy-five now.) I mention my hemoglobin is not too high. Dr. Raab decides to give me some iron. I ask could I have a glass of wine during chemo. "Yes, the day before and the day after. Not the day of it."

May 19, 1988—Mary Ann is here for Uncle Zoph's birthday. Linda Kinsey brings Barney Seigel's book on ex-

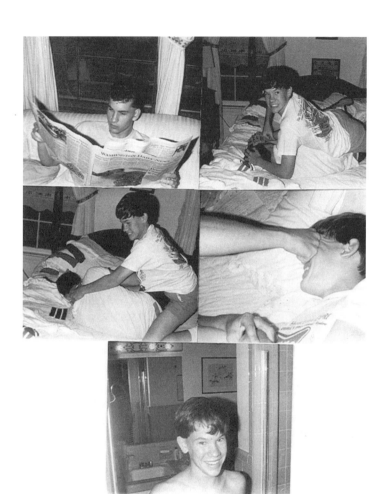

Reed and Morgan. Summer. 1988.

ceptional patients: there has never been a cancer that some-body hasn't lived through. Exceptional patients want to live more and do more. The quality of their lives gives them added life.

May 20, 1988—Friday. Zoph carries Freddie a birthday present. Morgan gets new contacts ordered.

May 21, 1988—Saturday. We're enjoying the cottage. Morgan, Zoph and I cook out. Morgan's trying to shape up academically. We talk about VES for him. I am trying to psyche up for chemo: a David and Goliath scenario.

May 22, 1988—We enjoy church and the river. I think I'm going to feel victorious through the chemo because I'm such a sunny, optimistic person with everything to live for, and how I know it, and how I keep reviewing and redoing to gear up my positive spirits.

May 23, 1988—Monday. Lisa Walker and Evelyn Smith are bringing supper tonight. Zoph and I go to the Oncology Department of Pitt Memorial Hospital for chemo. Marvene's away on a conference. A nurse invites Zoph in to be with me during the last few minutes of the hour. We stop by a boat that looks interesting on the way home. Then by a restaurant for a late lunch and home. I'm very sleepy. There's a sedative in the chemo. The nurse said I'd make it home before getting sick. It hit hard seven hours later. From 7:00 P.M. until 1:30 A.M. I was sick, sick, sick At 11:00 Zoph came upstairs. Seeing his face made me know I wanted to live.

May 24, 1988—Tuesday. I'm up and walking in Small-wood, but I'm weak and wish somebody would carry me home. I feel great, considering the book said I'd be sick three to four days. I go pick up Morgan's new contacts and enjoy seeing Mary Ruth Coleman home for the summer, but with UNC comps in June toward her doctorate. My appetite is off. Linda Kinsey visits. She helps a lot with the psychological pits. I'm deeply disappointed in my attitude.

15

May 25, 1988—Wednesday. Bill and Fran's 48th anniversary. Zoph, Morgan, Ryle, and I are going to dinner at Olivia and Riley's, but I can't stand up. I stay in bed. I'm sick, sick, and weak. I miss the party. Mouthwash, perfume, food—all aromas sicken me. Riley comes in, and he cries when he's been with me a little while . . . sort of after he asked me what I was reading. "A French book about a foreign exchange student." At that moment Olivia comes in, just finished with the spa.

May 26, 1988—Thursday. Zoph brings me a vanilla milkshake for breakfast. It's great. Riley brings me a vanilla milkshake for lunch. It's wonderful. I'm able to eat grapefruit sections. The liquid is delicious from the fruit. I'm walking by the P.M. with Ryle around Smallwood. Jan Hindsley brings macaroni. I devour it with pound cake.

May 27, 1988—Friday. We're off to the river cottage. I'm walking three miles a day again. I have a plate of spaghetti for lunch. I'm trying to gain back the seven pounds lost with chemo.

May 28, 1988—Saturday. We enjoy the cottage and the river.

May 29, 1988—Sunday. There is a reception at John Small, but I have to pace myself. Lenora and Eddie are here and buying a condo at Harbor Haven. Glenda and James visit. James thinks Zoph is his dad.

May 30, 1988—Monday. I'm feeling great and enjoying walking. The cards pour in: from Teresa and Woody Furlough, from Ceresy Jenkins and Ellen McCotter's class. . . . "I hope the lump by your heart gets better." One from Eastern has me on the operating table in a red gown.

May 31, 1988—Tuesday. Ashley Futrell is doing well after another bypass. I'm walking a lot as usual. About 45,000 women were sent for chemo last year. I don't know what percentage of them had cancer in the lymphs. I told Zoph that I might have the nerve to know after I've been cancer-free for five years. . . .

June 1, 1988—Wednesday. We're preparing for Reed's homecoming. I'd be in depression if it weren't for Linda Kinsey and Jane Wilson. They know hope and how to live high on it. Today Alice Daugherty had a Reach for Recovery group at her home. I don't want to go. A song on the radio upsets me at the last minute. Then I see Ann Dale Whitley in so much pain but showing up so gracefully.

June 2, 1988—Thursday. Ryle paints "Welcome Home Devil" (Blue Devil) on a banner. I do a "Congratulations VES Duke Champ" for the music room. Zoph picks them up at 11:00 (Westry, too).

Reach for Recovery Group Meeting
June 2, 1988

Hostess Alice Daugherty is very likable; laughs a lot; talks a lot.

1. Caroline Braddy—Son is leaving for Germany in June. Loved having an exchange student.
2. Barbara Fleming—41. Mastectomy in '87. Chemo. Husband has body shop. In bed for days with chemo. Daughter in college. Very sick with chemo. Had sedatives, and glucose before.
3. Anne Dale Whitley—Lives in Washington Park. Has red hair. Liver cancer. Called Lucy by uncle. Told not to walk. Wants to live. She looked at me. "Well, don't the best-looking people have cancer?" In pain . . . "The nicest people have cancer. The meanest ones don't." Jane Wilson: "They just give it to the rest of us."
4. To Etta Williams. From Farm Life. Awaiting body

Zoph and Robin

Beach Festival. 1988.

One week after surgery, tubes had been removed that morning_I was free to wear a slinky cocktail dress to the festival gala.

All hair had fallen out in the afternoon. Wigged Robin and Mother, Frances Roberson. June 6, 1988.

Riley and Olivia. June 6, 1988.

Dad's , Bill Roberson, 70th birthday. June 6, 1988.

From:
Bill Roberson

DEAR ROBIN,

YOUR DINNER LAST NIGHT WAS DELIGHTFUL. THANK YOU FOR EVERYTHING.

PLEASE NOTE THAT YOUR MOTHER & I GAVE OUR BALDWIN ORGAN ON 5/25 (A VERY SPECIAL DATE) TO THE CIVIC CENTER IN YOUR HONOR.

LOVE YOU!

DAD

6/7/85

Scott's Wharf
Main Street
Bath, N.C. 27808

strength for Duke. Bone marrow transplant. Taught. Cried. Overcame. Feels she's started all over in a way. She's on hold until her body's ready for the transplant. She wants desperately to live. She feels she'll make it. Her local doctors and nurses are super supportive.

5. Linda Mann—son, my student. Told would live seventeen months in 1981 . . . hip . . . Hodgkin's Disease. No cure. But a new protocol worked. Has lost hair three times. Her big goal was to live long enough for her toddler son to remember her. He's seven now.

6. Peggy Leggett—Operated on Friday, after me on Thursday. No lymph problem. Considering chemo. She looks scared.

7. Linda Kinsey—She has recruited all. Knows everyone's list.

8. Joyce Brooks—Mother of my former student Teresa . . . now a nurse. Wedding June 11. Joyce was told eleven years ago that there was no hope. She was seven months pregnant. Told to abort. She insisted on having the baby. Did chemo in Pollocksville. Is excited about the new bosom in time for the approaching twenty-fifth anniversary.

9. Becky Dawson—Mastectomy as of March four years ago . . . at four years old five or seven months, recurrence, had weaker chemo than I. But in March, to her horror—cancer—in the lining of the lungs. She's taking an oral chemo now and forever.

Two or three people echoed this opinion: Joyce—"I'm so much sweeter, a better person. I would choose to have the cancer back!"

I didn't want to go to the meeting. A radio song had upset me.

Barbara Fleming forgot about her wig, so she put the trash out anyway. A neighbor: "Hello, Alex."

June 11, 1988—Golf tournament. Fun dancing. Willises and Coiners were down. Sydna's working in Raleigh.

June 15, 1988—Wednesday. A fellow hoping his wife can take something for depression: "She's a couch potato all the time."

8:00 call from the hospital that the Muga test was awaiting me.

11:00 After the Muga. Now the chemo. I'm going to try to stay in these shorts and tennis shoes and do the exercise bike and work on Texas Gulf today and tomorrow.

Marvene: "We're going to try something different on you this time. I better explain it to your husband because you're going to be so sedated you won't know."

"Marvene, have you heard about the latest in cancer research? (Robin) Those breast cancer patients on chemo riding exercise bikes don't get sick with chemo." (Sterling Taylor called this news into me after reading it in—*The Bottom Line*—Bill's business newsletter.)

Marvene: "Patients who act sick don't do as well. Patients who don't exercise don't do as well."

Today I'll be taking Phenergan tablets—four every day for four days.

Weight: 134.5 Hooray! Perfect! No loss.

Passed heart check! Ned had told me there would be no problem with my little heart murmur. I never wanted to give up although I was pretty sick from 8:00 until 2:30, but time enough to keep sane and civil. I'm telling everybody it was a piece of cake this time. (And actually, comparatively, it was.) Jane Griffin and Mary Bilbro brought supper for my family.

June 16, 1988—Thursday. I feel up to a lot. I'm up and about at home. Zoph brought me Nutrament for breakfast and a milkshake for supper. Jeanne Lee and Alicia Sawyer brought supper for my family. Today is Bob McDonough's birthday.

June 17, 1988—Friday. Today is Phil Jr.'s birthday. I feel stronger, so we're moving to the cottage.

June 18, 1988—Saturday. The river life is wonderful. Zoph and I swim until time for the Greenville Ronald McDonald House Kickoff. Zoph is paired to play partners tomorrow with Michael Jordan. I sleep on the way home. I feel a little down, but that's because I'm still a little weak from chemo.

June 19, 1988—Sunday. It's Father's Day. We'll celebrate with my father next weekend. Olivia, Will, Walt, and I are off to see Zoph and Michael Jordan. I record it. One little boy, his mother told Michael, waited five- and one-half hours to see him. Zoph insisted I ride in his cart when the heat and walking took a toll on me. But I walked mostly and interviewed way-out Jack Boston, and Gary Jackson, Kelly, and Rusty Burkette, and closeups of the golfing gorilla. Zoph and Michael were four under par. They chat and laugh continuously.

I'm up at 1:00 A.M., 2:00 A.M., 3:00 A.M., etc. until 6:30 with fears, worries, and nightmares concerning Ryle's new friend Jarvis. Is he really a monster? I dreamed he was the golfing gorilla—my cancer—maybe I'm not going to live—my Master's—how can I get it done? Zoph says to wake him up next time to talk it out. Oh, plus the perennial pressure in a drum scene, which is an anxiety attack that I've had before about half a dozen times. Ryle's sleeping in the hammock unnerves me. I'm awake on guard for fear someone's coming in on us or on her. Maybe this night can be blamed on Ativan withdrawal.

June 20, 1988—Ashley Futrell's Greenville oral surgeon

left a tooth in him that was supposed to have been extracted, so Ashley's been suffering needlessly.

Rosebud enjoys the roses that Jim Blanton brings to her from the BCC Memorial Garden. I play the piano while Martha, "Bubbles," sings. I feel keyed up. Kay Buckman, Sara Katherine, and Cameron bring us a spaghetti supper. I sleep much better, but not normally.

June 29, 1988—Tuesday. Mae has surgery, a mastectomy today. She does great. We send her a cascading plant called Bridal Veil. I stay home waiting for Marvene to help and feeling neglected by her because she doesn't return my 8:00 call until 5:00. I keep calling her, though, just hoping there is somebody who can suggest a medicine for my allergic reaction to Adriamycin. When Alice McClure calls, I figure she'll sympathize with me since she says I'm in her heart and she has some pies for me. So I tell her that I'm embarrassed to go out of the house, that my face is rashed over, that of all times I'm invited to the Coral Bay. So what does my friend say to comfort me? "Everybody will say, 'There's Robin Potts. And she looks like hell.' " I laugh the rest of the day . . . and anytime I think of Alice. Marvene calls. I start Cortisone cream and Chlor-Trimeton.

Linda Kinsey calls to tell me she had been thinking about me during chemo. The power of one friend's positive thinking!

June 22, 1988—Wednesday. Today is Hannah and James's forty-second anniversary. I was in their wedding at age three. Hannah calls to thank me for the plant present, and I tell her I remember what a stinker I was in her wedding—not going down the aisle with the bridesmaids, but instead with her and my Daddy, Bill. She says she's loved me for what I am. She's always been remarkable. I told her I would send a friend who needed a marriage role model to study the Hannah-James union. Hannah: "It's not easy. Tell her to come, though, and I'll show her how to do it."

My rash is sinking in—retrenching.

Mother calls. Uncle Phil is seriously sick with liver cancer.

June 23, 1988—Thursday. Anger is welling up in me. Why didn't Ned discover my tumor earlier if it had been there maybe one and one-half years? Mae's "no lymph" situation provoked my feelings. Why couldn't I have been finished with the ordeal with the mastectomy, too? Zoph says, "Maybe your tumor wasn't detectable. It just wasn't big enough to show. But then Phil said it was the good, slow-growing kind. Well, how the hell did it get in the lymphs then?"

I'm imagining Ned feels anguished that he couldn't have detected it.

Claire calls to give us a ham. Zoph has WDLX coming the wedding weekend and my treatment week. Maybe we can figure it out. . . . How to entertain with no bother or time due to chemo and a wedding. Russ had advised Reed to return to VES for sports reasons. Claire told me how impressed she is that Russ would consider Reed's welfare above all.

Dr. Fearing and Dr. Allen are eager to help guide me in my comps paper. My Master's started spring of 1986 and expires spring of 1991. I'm finishing (really not even to the middle of) Luke's work now—Texas Gulf at the moment. In January I'll take my comps. Dr. McMillan sends his concern for my health. Dr. Fearing: "As tough as you are, I know you'll be fine." Dr. McMillan says he'll waive the foreign-language exam. He told Dr. Fearing: "We have to trust our own foreign language majors."

Me: "Dr. Fearing, this year's perfect for me to do my paper and exams. I have a year off from teaching. I'm sick too much from chemo to keep up in a regular graduate course."

Dr. Fearing: "I agree. It's perfect. It'll give you something to do."

Me: "Do you think it makes sense?"

Dr. Fearing: "Yes. It's something you want to do. It's therapy."

July 12, 1988—Tuesday.* (Talking to Riley and Olivia) Larry Windley is home for the weekend from Carolina. I walk out on the flagstone terrace in the park house to find a note: "Chère Madame, I have a wild friend from UNC coming Thursday. Would you go out with him?" I tell Larry that I am flattered, but that I am going with Zoph and I recommend Judy Dudley (because she is in the same neighborhood and is convenient. I am bemused that Larry is not aware that Zoph and I have been married for twenty-six years). In telling this to Riley and Olivia, I mention: "I have three cribs up." Olivia questions: "Three cribs?" I reply: "Yes, three cribs. There's this one for———, and that one for———, and ———?" Then I realize that I must have forgotten a baby. Riley covers for me. "That crib's for the baby." "Yes," I say. "That one's for the baby." But what is the baby's name? Is it a he or she? Oh, no! I have no clue! I go to the hospital. I tell the nurses: "I've been involved with my surgery." (This was a cover-up; I've really been doing my ECU graduate work!) They say that's been no problem and that they understand. I start changing a baby: She turns into a forty-year-old woman who tells me she is not my baby. Then I go to the nurse who hands over my baby girl. She has been in the hospital since last spring. (It's the next spring because I'm wearing Bermuda shorts.) The "baby" is wearing

---

*A dream of July 12, 1988. Zoph and I laughed a lot over this.

a plaid big-collared school dress and her legs hang to my knees. Her shoes are brown leather with straps, at least size 5, maybe 7's. She spent Christmas in the hospital, of course. The nurses assure me that that was no problem—they presented her with gifts. One was her shoes. Relief! That vague knowing I'd forgotten something important is gone. I hope Olivia didn't notice.

The after-chemo problems have crystallized. I feel like I've arrived because I'm now sick five minutes, down from seven hours. Three chemos down now—swelling in chemo hand—take—a rash begins the sixth day—take—upset stomach—take—sore throat.

July 4, 1988—Saturday. The weakness sets in the fifth day. Oh, Lord! Ken's wedding brunch. Then WDLX! But Butterball's catering was great and I didn't lift a finger, just swam and chatted. Marvene says to stop swimming in the river. (Go to the pool.)

July 15, 1988—Friday. Uncle Zoph died during the night. Jerry Bron and Mary Ann will have a jazzy musicale as an inspirational memorial funeral Sunday at 2:00. Mary Ann will use our townhouse to receive family and friends. Since Uncle Zoph didn't know anything or anybody—hasn't for the past week—I am relieved that he is released . . . that joyful, blithe, witty, warm, wonderful man. He has made an indelible impact on us—on all my children. We are indebted to him, and I hope we can carry his spirit forever . . . his thirst for life at its best.

July 16, 1988—Saturday. Caribbean islands. Tonight "Chez Cheri" at St. Martin's. The waiters are juking while they serve.

July 17, 1988—Sunday. We fly for seventeen minutes to St. Bart's. At lunch Ann and George Miller come in with hugs. (They're sunburned, they say, everywhere, from Saline Beach.) We dined together at Manopany—the trumpeter plays from a pad in the pool—the palm trees sway. I finish a foot of a glass of strawberry daiquiri. A couple from Atlanta who are married one week say, "What an effort," when we mention our twenty-five-year marriage.

July 18, 1988—Monday. We tour, Zoph driving the Moke up the hills and cliffs. We dine with the Millers at Les Trois Gourmands—pink flatware—pink accessories—glass-white tile floor—linens. The restaurant was closed the night before because, as the concierge says, *"J'étais fatiguée."*

French. Catherine at Chez Francine's: Her husband is an international banker. They have a two-bedroom apartment in Manhattan plus a maid's quarters. An apartment in Paris. A house in St. Bart's, where she has come for seventeen years. Her son (going into his senior year) starts the conversation with us. She says St. Bart's is special because it doesn't have tour people—that she likes for her son to keep up his French via St. Bart's. Catherine enjoys talking, especially to Zoph, her husband has just left after two and one-half weeks. She keeps fooling with her neckline, sort of pulling it up. She recommends that we rent. She rents her house. She suggests the Sabine rental company, which will give us a tour of all rentable homes. She looks like Catherine de Neuve, only she's about thirty-nine. She finishes talking. She tells us that her father (her parents live in Paris now) was an international banker. She grew up in Panama, Buenos Aires, New York, and Paris. Catherine: "If you can live in New York, you can live anywhere. The people are cold there and everything is difficult." She said it took her a year to cope with New York. She takes her leave: "Maybe I'll see you again." She steps out of her clothes when she reaches the sand. Zoph bought a zoom lens as soon as possible.

We swim in clear Caribbean seas.

July 19, 1988—Tuesday. We celebrated our twenty-

27

St. Bart's. Caribbean Sea. Summer. 1988.

St. Bart's. Caribbean Sea. Summer. 1988.

St. Bart's. Caribbean Sea. Summer. 1988.

sixth anniversary. We tour. We swim at Saline. We dine at Ghanahani. White linens. Music. Sea breeze. Charming waiters.

At Faleos we enjoy a New York couple. She: "I've lived in New York all my life, and I feel I've earned out . . . the retail business is bad off."

July 20, 1988—Wednesday. We fly from St. Bart's to St. Martin's. At St. Martin's, we shop for the WDLX girls. I buy a solar calculator; Zoph, a zoom lens.

In the shower I find a lump in my right armpit. Terror. Zoph says it could be a cyst or a natural sign of a temporary infection.

We dine at Cheri's, where the waiters are juking. Live music. Zoph compliments the manager who says: "We work hard on the atmosphere."

We're having such a fun time. If we're offered a chance to be bumped off the plane tomorrow, we'll do it!

August 3, 1988—Mother and Daddy and I are off to Duke today to see Dr. Gregory Georgaide. Linda says he's very conscientious and kind, and to describe her and her best wishes to him. She gives me a cue with kind, well-meaning people who say, "You look so good." Launch another subject on the split second.

Cousin Doris Rodgers may use Morgan on the tractor or in landscaping.

Reed has football at 5:00 and yards to do this morning.

I hope Marvene can line up Phil to get me into physical therapy.

Lunch at the Governor's Inn, with Mother and Daddy—seafood and piano music. Daddy is in bad back pain whenever he stands up from sitting or reclining. Pinched nerve in the lower back. His orders are not to sit—to walk—to use only a straight-backed chair.

From Dr. Gregory Georgaide—is kind and says one

protocol is as good as another—we transfer to Dr. McCardy—a hematologist and endocrinologist who can best answer our questions. Am I on the best protocol?

"Yes. Unequivocally. I recommend reconstruction one month after chemo. Dr. Georgaide does beautiful work."

To me: "You are always going to be their baby. This is traumatic. It is very serious, but the decision for surgery was excellent. The results are by far much better. Dr. Raab is a very special person. She does work for us down in that area. Her surgery is excellent. As much as I'd like to say that we do the best, it's as good as she would get here, and we're pretty good."

Fran: "It's so shocking. So shocking."

Dr. McCardy: "She should have a long and happy life. Of course, there are risks. What she is taking is very toxic, but there are no guarantees in life. The tumor could recur, and we could treat it. We've decided on reconstruction for you after all chemo is over. March."

Fran: "Isn't it wonderful that they can do this? We couldn't rest until we came here."

Dr. McCardy: "You should have taken her to Italy."

Fran: "We liked Paris better."

Dr. McCardy: "The world has really changed."

To me alone: "I think your folks like you."

Dr. McCardy: "You picked the right doctor down there."

Me: "I think I picked the right doctor in you."

After a day at Duke Medical Center, Daddy made us laugh as he described himself searching for his parking ticket: "Even a blind pig can find an acorn sometime."

Daddy to me: "Aren't you glad to know that everything your doctors have done hasn't been wrong? I mean, they could have told us that today."

August 11, 1988

Dear Colonel and Madame Berthier,

I hope that you are doing well. In May you graciously gave my parents immeasurable pleasure. I want to thank you for your singular, charming hospitality. My parents speak often of their extraordinary memories. Of all the large cities visited, Paris is their favorite.

Zoph and I flew to St. Bart's island in the Caribbean two weeks ago to celebrate our twenty-fifth anniversary one year late. Last year we were too busy (with a young visitor from Strasbourg who was with our family for four weeks. Charles, my son, who is the age of Jean-Marc, has the opportunity to visit there). Please give my best to Jean-Marc, Beatrice, Karine, Chantal, and Jean-Pierre. Charles thinks often about a career with the government as a fish and wildlife inspector. Today I'm going to collect some required information on these positions. Now, as you perhaps know, he is in the Coast Guard: this will last two more years.

My parents hope that you received some books that they sent you in May. They spoke with their friend Linda about Beatrice. She and her young daughters are hoping that Beatrice will come to the U.S. to their home. I am disappointed that we could not have Beatrice last summer, but maybe in the future Beatrice can come.

Since May I have been thinking so often of you that now I've finally decided to write to you about my challenge. If you were in my situation, I would like to know it because I love you. Well, please sit down. First of all, know that I am doing fine, and my prognosis is excellent. But when my parents were in Italy after their visit with you, my doctor told me to have surgery immediately. After surgery May 5, she told me to have chemo every three weeks for six times. Then rest for six months. Then in March, a continuation of three or four treatments. Then in April, I will have reconstructive surgery. We think that this therapy will prohibit a return of the malignancy . . . (in May my malignancy was in the breast and lymphs). But what a shock for my poor parents. On their

33

arrival from Europe, my brother and my sister-in-law met them at the airport to tell them of my condition.

This week my parents took me to a famous medical center called Duke University. There the doctors reassured them that my surgery was excellent and the choice of chemo was excellent; that although there are some risks with this therapy, and the malignancy can return (in this case the doctors would treat it again), I should have a long and happy life. The anguished faces of my parents changed with hope and assurance. My father was a member of the hospital board for this medical center, and he and my mother would not have been able to have any rest until they had taken me for the opinion of specialists.

I asked my principal for this year off. The therapy weakens my resistance to germs, so I can't be around children with colds, and I won't have my normal energy for a week after treatments. Already he has replaced me with a Spanish teacher. I will use this year to continue my individual studies at the university at my own speed.

Next summer Zoph and I want to celebrate our anniversary in Scotland (an old dream of my husband's). But during this visit, why not a little visit across the English Channel?

France will be too close not to visit Dinard. It's logical to me. When you come to our little town, I want to take you by boat from here to the ocean for beautiful sights.

Today Morgan, who is fifteen, continues his driver's training and begins the piano; Reed, who is sixteen, continues to practice soccer; Ryle, who is twenty-five, is decorating store windows, waiting tables, and teaching in a day care; Charles serves as a Coast Guard officer; Zoph runs the radio station—he enjoys this. Zoph and I are looking forward to a visit to Washington, D.C. in September to attend a radio conference.

It's wonderful to have life. In my life you have a special part.

With deep affection,
Robin

August 15, 1988—Dear Mae,

I'm looking forward to seeing you and your mother on Wednesday at our dedication of Rosebud's rose garden. Your energy beamed my way energizes us all as well as doing magic. Your first book held my mother still while she was in shock about me. We were slowly turning the beautiful pages together while trying to decide how to go to the next step with doctors. That book was a Godsend.

Your next gorgeous book is a Godsend in a different way—with our children. Charles, at twenty-one, spent last year stationed in Alaska with the Coast Guard. This year he requested Coinjock, N.C. The only exciting thing he has at the moment are memories. So here comes your gorgeous scenes of Alaska plus the rest of the country with a fascinating essay on us as a people.

Last Wednesday my parents took me to Duke for a review of my case. Dr. Kenneth McCardy, Jr. assured them that my surgery was excellent as is the protocol I'm following—and that, although there are risks (the tumor could recur, at which time they would treat it again)—I should have a long and happy life.

My last of the first six chemos is September 1—then I'm off for six months. Then in March, three or four more chemos. Then after a month, I'll go to Duke for reconstructive surgery.

I've taken this year off from teaching—there's lots I want to do through ECU—no formal classes for credit, but individual studies toward my Master's in Business and Technical Writing. Also, a Review in French Grammar to audit.

My mother is so strong and whatever I need her to be. At her condominium a couple of weeks ago, we all danced until 12:30 and had a smashing time. But earlier we were all dressing, and for some reason she came to my bathroom door talking. I then cracked the door to hear her better. Then I realized I didn't have on my hair. I said, "Oh no! I'm sorry! I didn't mean to shock you! I forgot I didn't have it on!" Mother (with a knowing smile on her face): "That's all right. I've seen you before with no hair."

Mae, we had a fabulous weekend with them at the beach. And I have a lot of beautiful things to tell you about St. Bart's. The white-tiled, pink flatware restaurant; the seafood and vegetables arranged like flowers on our plates; the trade winds' constant breeze; the thirty- and sixty-foot Catamarans in the harbor—big as Vikings—the gorgeous swimming, French everywhere, the spectacular flights in and out, the "Belafonte" music—we're really rotten.

Thank you for being my mother when she was in Italy during the first of these traumatic months. I'm riding (Daddy got me one after hearing that chemo patients with breast cancer who ride don't get sick) a Schwinn Air Dyne Bike ten miles a day and feel splendid. (Just weak the week after chemo.) I have my fifth chemo tomorrow, Thursday, August 16, 1988.

Thank you for buoying my will and sanity.

Much love,
Robin

September 15, 1988—to Washington, DC

15 September, Thursday
Program Director, Gary Jackson
Riley—VP Sales
Zoph—President
Olivia—Guide—tickets to Kennedy Center
Van—Hurricane news: Gilbert

Lunch outside DC—soup and salad. Waitress is Ryle's age. Grand Hyatt, one year old, old charm. Pianist playing in a pool. Mauve. Marble. "Do you have any change, Ma'am?" Shops—Woodie's—11's. Tall kindly efficient cool clerking during a sale. Wig. Parties. Conversation. Mary Ellen McCarthy and Jack from Raleigh—daughter in Boca—not a place for *children*—all spoiled. Daughter's husband, stockbroker; "Maybe they'll move when the children get in school. It's not the real world. Drugs. Problems."

To the old post office—party—outside elevator—tour bells. Rae isn't there—another guide. "Do you know Rae to all guides?" "Yes. She's coming back to work tomorrow." Music by James Taylor's brother—charming, mellow, then kicky, touching sense of the moment. Take a wrong turn walking, leaving about 11:00. Scary. Street people. Sleeper sidewalk Reed's build. After midnight, lady in Bicentennial Building gives us a number to call taxi on pay phone (We're not supposed to hear; then she laughs that that will take a lot of coins). The number doesn't work. She tells us to walk to Seventh and stand for a taxi. Then she says it's too dangerous as we leave. She doesn't really care.

Dim streets. Darkness. No taxis. Olivia's baby feet hurting. Gary and Riley talking or praying and joking. Street corner people. Bars. Loud talking. Scared. Taxi driver—young, black, curly haired, short cut style, bright-eyed, and a little whiskey, talkative, bubbly: "Worrier you from? That's not bad. You guys would never have made it past the shelter. Don't walk here! I don't unless I have to. I carry a knife. I'm not violent unless I have to be. I go with the flow. Don't go past Thea. You're in a bad part of town. I'm in with the hookers. After 3:00 I'm always busy with the hookers."

"Aren't they afraid they'll catch something?"—Olivia.

"Your wallet."

"Thanks. Take care."

"Have you heard of———? I know you have. He used to be a street person. Now he's got a million, and he doesn't do anything. Money changes people. Money talks."

1:00 A.M.—Sleep.

Breakfast. Bellhop. 8:10.

Me: "Good morning. What is the hurricane doing?"

"It isn't ready yet."

"Has the hurricane hit Mexico?"

"That hasn't come in to the office, Ma'am. But when it arrives, I will have the office call you. Enjoy your breakfast."

Olympian walking with Olivia. Whistles from high-up construction workers. Radio man is passing. "That must have made you feel good to be whistled at in jogging clothes. . . . I mean shorts, of course, but jogging clothes."

Saturday. Shopping.

P.M.—Kennedy Center. Gilbert & Sullivan. Sullivan died first, a bachelor.

Gilbert: "I can't go on without a Sullivan, and I can't find another one."

Gilbert died saving a child in a lake.

Sullivan: "We are writing and writing to feel more alive."

Operetta: Gilbert & Sullivan are the characters of the drama, and are virtually discovered writing, singing, or at

38

least rehearsing their own material. A rollicking comedy in which the Gilbert and Sullivan songs are used. Within the play Fritz Weaver (Gilbert) and Noel Harrison (Sullivan) conduct rehearsals at the Savoy Theater for a command concert for Queen Victoria. There are excerpts from eight or so operettas. The aging Sullivan will be carrying on with a twenty-three-year-old and Sullivan's pal, the Duke of Edinburgh, will get to sing some Gilbert & Sullivan for his mum. True enough, if exaggerated.

Almost every lyricist has at some time or another proclaimed his indebtedness to W.S. Gilbert. I laughed until I cried.

Sunday. Riley's birthday, Forty-second. Bellhop: Mom is Doris Weston on the County Board of Education. "Are you all from Bath? You make me homesick. Have you got room for me? Been here eight years. . . . "

The Kennedy Center: The concept of a national cultural center in Washington was first introduced more than twenty-five years ago. At that time the city had a cultural life, but no major auditorium for its local orchestra, opera company, or theater groups, much less for major touring companies from other U.S. cities or abroad. It is a cultural melting pot. On September 25 the Open House will present more than sixty performing groups and individual artists on the stage and public spaces of the center for a one-day free extravaganza that annually attracts more than 50,000 people, sponsored by the Friends of the Kennedy Center. The open house dramatizes Washington's remarkable artistic diversity by showcasing Country and Western singers, blues, Caribbean, and Latin American ensembles, African heritage dancers, Japanese Koto players, pop and classical vocalists, and modern dance troupes—all of whom call the Washington area home.

October 25, 1988—Mr. Francisco. Lucy and I at ECU

39

Travel Series. Sellout: *Time-Life.*Ben Franklin—first ambassador to France. Ernest Hemingway—F. Scott Fitzgerald. James Whistler sold his mother to Paris. Art Buchwald. 17 Boulevards—l'Etoile. Eiffel—two years to put up tower. Coat flyer—Barnum was ready with an offer. Obelisk—symbolizes agreement among men. Café—sit long enough and you'll see someone you know. Thomas Jefferson—once envoy to France. Early 1900 travel film—ladies could smoke and learn all those continental rage dances. The can-can (mild precision tumbling)! Gloria Swanson—huge sunken bath. Lindbergh—twenty-five years old. Parade day after. 1944—Liberation. Normandy. Omaha Beach. Saint Germain Church—the oldest in Paris. Jerome Kern & Oscar Hammerstein—"The Last Time I Saw Paris." Gershwin—*An American in Paris.* Cole Porter bet Gershwin 1,000 francs that he couldn't play the piano without being recognized. Picasso held court in the cafés. Many painters paid with paintings. Tender is the night—open-air book stalls. James Fenimore Cooper—*Last of the Mohicans.* 400,000 objects in the Louvre. Henry IV built Place de Visages. Rodin Museum. About 2,000 women in the world can afford to buy something from Paris. About 6,000 families live and work on the Seine. Versailles—construction began when Louis XVI was twenty-three—36,000 workers at a time; 14,000 fountains—mile-long lake. Peace treaty for World War I. Rockefeller helped restore it. White added to French flag by Lafayette. All of Lafayette's descendants are honorary citizens of the U.S. We say to them: "Parisians, you do our croissants and we'll do your plumbing." Helena Rubenstein—interested in beauty and banking: "I had to pay the bills for all those starving widows." Fontainebleau—forty miles from Paris. Pope Pius held here until he agreed to annul Napoleon's marriage to Josephine. John Paul Jones, after the Revolution, died destitute in Paris, honored in Paris one century after his death. Josephine Baker—the only woman to have a 21-gun salute. 1,700 ducks.

Halloween. Winston-Salem. Radio state convention. AM panel discussion. Leaders: Dave Lingerfelt, Newton: Jim Childress, Hickory. Nonstop Chapel Hill concept. Good bargains in AM. "If a cow breaks its leg in Granville County, that's news in Granville County." That builds an audience. Trading post. Obituaries. Perception is what counts (not Arbitron)! It's drive. Get sales people who believe in the product! We're information. It's in the home. Sales power. Get outside the station! Have the high school students come in to do the show and commercials. Don't try to compete with FM. Promote. Get the public talking about your AM station! Have a promotion every day! Doug: two full time people to do AM Panel: Need no less than five or six people. AM in High Point does over $100,000 annually. Audience: Sam—Can't have AM & FM in the same building. We have to work 3 to 4 times as hard. It's not easy to do AM. Don't automate! Difficult production. "You've got a problem. The company has decided to push FM—like FM is an afterthought." Programming: "I'd rather put my ads with you because you're more into automation—let some syndication control your programming." The AM competition is cable. Frequency is the most important factor in results! We bombard with 2,000 a day. "Big agency: 1,000 to spend. 10 by 100 ads. The point is to get 100 commercials. Even with a smaller audience, the AM is the most cost efficient! We don't sell results. We sell *response*. I sell you the time and *give you the promotion*. Know your facts on cable. Prove that 75 percent of viewing is tradition. Twenty-five percent watch HBO, seven to eight percent watch cable. Prove at any one time watching. What quality: a twenty-five-inch screen or ours is as big as yours. Production? Oh, they (the TV people). Fine. That's what it looks like. Develop a personality outside of music. AM is fun radio. Video show commercials—two and one half minutes. What's new with birthdays. Nursing home—Social worker records spotlights and the nursing home pays for it. Make it tangible. Take the client a cassette of their commercial. Introduction by Jim:

Dr. Dick Levin—A marvelous treat. One of the most charismatic people you can find. Professor of Business Strategy. Consultant. (Duke, Exxon). We all know a consultant is a guy who knows a hundred ways to make love but knows no girls. He's written more books than most of us have read. He makes more learning happen in an hour than anybody.

Top Management Visibility
Meet our president
Dukes like to talk to Kings
At least a note from the president

Miscellaneous
What kind of miracle needed
Every salesperson

Needs to consult
A consulting mind set
Knowledge of the customer's business
Risk taking/problem solving
Selling skills

Dick Levin—Atlantic Beach.
Ryle—Needs to know the customer's needs and present them.
Radio. Vital to the growth of the economics of the area. Change, difficult. Example: move the coffee machine. In 1974, GM makes ten business assumptions that will carry. What got us here won't get us there. We over-

came with management. The one thread: successful leaders, insatiable appetite. Pooh! "I'm from Kentucky—so just about everything is difficult for me until I've spent some time on it."

Training
New business development
Game plan
First priority of management is to teach
New RAB sales training course
Media fragmentation
Map strategies
Target Audience
Two hundred and forty more radio stations in past eight years
See knowledge is power

In the Olympics—athletes would win by 1/100 of a second (the difference was by the fire in the belly—the passion).

Sir Edmund Hillary—to conquer Mount Everest—Saluted for efforts in Parliament. (Six teammates died.) Ran down the aisle kicking the portrait of the mountain—"You beat me, but I'm not finished growing." Months later he climbed it.

Great ideas:

Closings (charge for bad weather)
Special gifts for Christmas (for a commercial)
Direct mail
Sky Diving—client prize
Radio Parade (sponsors buy whatever . . . example: jets)
Rotating car promo
Yellow Pages

Help-wanted ads
Go the extra mile
Ads for blueberry pickers (May-October)
Ads for migrants (even in Spanish) (eighty percent of these
    people do not speak English)
Also tell in Spanish of legal and medical help
Help for manufacturers
Ads for sewing machine operators
Weather line (one year–25,000 calls for a station)
Prepared spots from an auto dealer advertising products
    when temperatures run below 32 degrees
Benefit dances for the Rescue Squad
You got a problem? You call us!
Make the public feel the station is their station
Leave employment applications at factories
Contest: Match the song with the business
High illiteracy rate: newspapers don't work

November 6, 1988—Foreign Language Conference. Saturday. Why Foreign Language—Elementary School? U.S.

1. Commerce
2. Travel (ignorance looks arrogant)
3. World peace & understanding
4. Tolerance
5. Economics (Japan has 10,000 businesspeople in U.S. speaking English. U.S. has 100 businesspeople in Japan speaking Japanese)
6. Research
7. To communicate to each other—a growing Hispanic population
8. Nurses, Social Workers: A social service
9. Jobs—Increased opportunity—secretary, fast food

Michelle, Robin, Hannah, Kay. Noël. 1988.

Michelle, Robin, Mary Ann. Ryle. Kay. Noël. 1988.

Robin and Will. Noël. 1988.

Reed and Morgan. Noël. 1988.

Reed, Will, Morgan, Charles. Noël. 1988.

Mother and Dad, Robin, Rose and Jane. Noël. 1988.

10. Broaden goals
11. Migrant Workers
12. Foreign investors
13. Enrichment
    Because a child is going to stay in a small place doesn't mean his/her mind should be small.
14. Extends IQ
15. Fun
16. Listening Skills
17. Relatives
18. Develops Native English

- Working with a translator is like talking with a mouthful of feathers.
- Idea: That the U.S. will never declare war on a country that Americans can't find on the map.
- People no longer are giving us translation. Scientist can't read information journals to support research.
- High School student: making six dollars supervising migrants
- Tyrrell County—the largest county—only two schools
- One out of three farmland acres provides an export crop
- One out of six manufacturing jobs depends on foreign markets. Most of our foreign tobacco is sold in foreign markets.
- In one's native language, one only has to listen about half the time. Children need to listen and work harder and there is a carryover to other subjects.
- Research on long achievement: three possibilities: 1. Worry that test scores will go down. 2. Worry that nothing happens to achievement (something for nothing attitudes, broaden horizons). 3. Achievement goes up.

Spills over. *Every* child involved. The dignity of human thought is increased.

Christmas 1988—Forty-some family and friends for Christmas Brunch. The Foodland Deli did a tenderloin & ham biscuits—terrific.

December 1988—Carrying the accordion sprained my back—concerts to Barbara Mantz's class and talk on Noel on France and Mondays at the nursing home caroling—all forty-five folks in all rooms. A bone scan and X ray suggest December 15 that nothing else is going on in the way of a recurrence of a tumor—it must be just a sprain. I can't lift anything.

Late January, 1989—Wig goes! With one inch of hair! To Kathyrn Cooper's wedding dance as hosts sans wig. To the mall record bar, the clerk: "Oh, New Wave!"

February 1989—First week. Feels like bursitis in the right shoulder. X rays and bone scan confirm nothing's going on in the way of recurrent malignancy.

February 1989—First week. Zoph and I enjoy Key West, Naples, and Palm Beach with radio folks. In April, Allison will give me physical therapy to get my upper body in shape. Lifting anything hurts. My shoulder pains (Motrin).

March 23, 1989—Today is Jane Griffin's birthday, fortieth. Bought her *The Big Chill* with the California Raisin song. Nancy McLean calls to ask me to speak for the Cancer Crusade Banquet. I can speak on appreciation and how uplifting Cancer Crusaders are. The second protocol of chemo started last Thursday, March 16, which was to be a piece of cake. Sick until 4:00 A.M. plus next day. Next time I'll know to take Ativan two days before and have it put in my chemo. At the chamber banquet, Bill Zachman was honored and "undone." Reed just mailed one hundred five dollars for the beach week deposit for Taylor Whichard, Kevin Westbrook, Greg Rayburn, Mike Mizelle, David Jones, Denny Hawkins,

Morgan, Reed. Russ Darrow. Noël.1988.

Robin and Ryle. Noël. 1988.

Ryle and Kay. Noël. 1988.

Zoph and Robin. Noël. 1988.

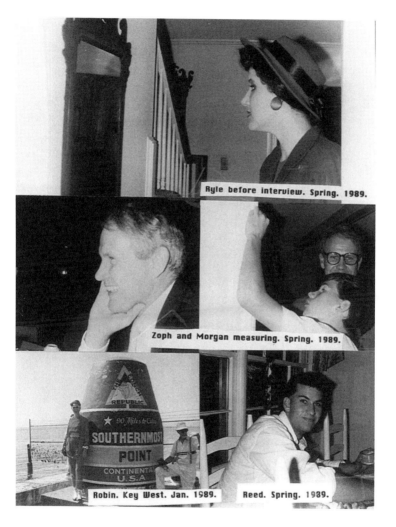

Ryle before interview. Spring. 1989.

Zoph and Morgan measuring. Spring. 1989.

Robin. Key West. Jan. 1989.

Reed. Spring. 1989.

Mark Brookshire, Tim Warner, and himself.—Morgan danced in *The Music Man* with Cindy Christiano Thursday, Friday, and Saturday. Terrific. Michael Bilbro, mayor.—Linda Kinsey leaves tomorrow, March 23, 1989 for reconstruction. I missed the support group luncheon at P.J.'s; sick. It was only the third day after chemo.—One of the painters heard me say Thursday I was going to lie down, that I had just had chemo. Monday he tells me a success story: His cousin had Hodgkin's.—Bunk told the painter no liquor, seafood, or pork, to combat gout.—Walking in the cemetery March 15, the day before chemo; I.B. prays for me as I leave, says he and Josephine are available night and day. Thursday when I was so sick I thought of them. I didn't feel guilty for wanting to die because I knew they were pulling for me to live. They were heartening to think about—their strength!—It's heartening to see at Charlie Tom's Jan Hasty, Wanda Johnson, Mary Alice Smith, and Chris Ayers, on her birthday, organizing for the Cancer Crusade—Dr. Raab is heartening. She waved to me across the expanse at ECU. Zoph and I were thrilled with the NC & ECU Symphonies playing *The Planets* by Gustav Holst—I'll look for heartening stories to tell the Crusade crowd.

March 23, 1989—Thursday, 8:00. The CNN News: Terrorist possibilities of attacking an American plane in Europe during Easter. Reed and I hear this as we are on the way to meet the AIFS group in the mall for Raleigh and Flight 588 Pan Am from New York at 6:30. The State Department assures AIFS and me that all is go, but be careful to allow extra time for security at the airport.—My counts are low, but should start up. A Mrs. Julian Jackson in Dr. Raab's waiting room: "Julian Jackson lived next door to the Robersons at Old Ford. As neighbors, they would help each other out. Susan, the mother of eleven (my great-grandmother), would make wonderful biscuits every morning. Julian liked to eat over there. He did a lot. They helped each other with to-bacco. Made their lard about once a year. All the children worked. Everybody. Raised their own chickens. Rosa called us one time; she heard Julian was sick. Tell her hello. We live out near Jamesville. I've been bringing Julian up here two years now. He can't hear well. He's eighty-three. The doctor says he does real well, considering what he's got and his age.

I feel furious that cancer has struck this young pretty stylish lady I see here with her husband—10:00. During NBA commercials, Morgan showcases Bobby McFerrin for me, an interview plus some of his songs and video, fabulous fun free spirit.

March 24, 1989 Friday—Linda Kinsey's in surgery now, reconstruction, at Duke. A mom from the AIFS chain calls: The group landed in Amsterdam at 6:30 this morning. Jo Lewis comes with flowers at 12:30. All her kids are coming in. She's recuperating from playing a seventy-five-page so-nata last weekend, then visiting her growing up home in South Carolina. "Mother died, so it's just not home any-more. I have an old-maid, sixty-seven-year-old sister. She's in her own world. I couldn't get her to come for Easter. She lives with her animals in a fourteen-room house."—Whenever I'm qualmy about probably not having a future, I think of Jim Ferrell: What he wouldn't give to have this after-noon—this morning—this meal with his family—this con-versation. And I recharge my spirit.

April 1989—From Jerry Bron's sermon: "The Morning View of Life": "That is what the faith is about. The morning after, the new view of things, the recognition that sets the darkness aglow with possibility, the knowledge that noth-ing, not even death itself, can separate us from the love of God. (Me: Here I have to whittle it to mean a love of life, of creation.) . . . Prayer: "Father (I have to whittle this because

51

to me no father could let happen what happens to people, so I think of a deistic creator who started us off and now we're on our own) for all the light which illuminates the days of our earthly journey, we give you thanks." These thoughts gird me, reinforce my love of life, and appreciation for guiding lights along the way.

April 7, 1989 Friday. I just happened to be on a bar stool next to him, and he needed to talk. Zoph was talking sports three people away. Zoph and I leave for Durham at 2:30. His friends are interesting and stimulating and fun. There's one leech, (no, he's not a leech, he's lonely), but maybe he won't be around where I am. He was attracted to me. He was very lonely.—Why is my hair falling out again? But more to the point: I want to complain, to bitch, but I shouldn't have time to do that. I'm going to be all finished with chemo in a matter of weeks, next Thursday, the 13th; then, if my counts are up, the 29th, if not, a week later. I hope I'm keeping my contract with my Maker. I hope I'm on track and growing and maturing. I hope I'm not babying my spirit. Last night at Connie's birthday party, I enjoyed her sisters, Betty and Bobbie: "Connie was always the beautiful one, with dark hair she could sit on; I was bald!" She has opinions of men: "They are nice, nicer than women, and steady, and industrious and they take orders. I think women are messier because they were never Marines."—Bet said her father's hell was World War II when he was stuck at Dupont with only women, and they wouldn't mind him.—Dr. Garringer was a country doctor. Hilda (parents of Connie, Bobbie, Betty): "We were paid in chickens—and we didn't have a coop. We always had a half a dozen cakes." Bobbie: "The biggest time I had was going to a friend's house. I rode on the bus with her because Mother would never have let me go, and seeing her dirt floor, it was great, I thought—and the outside toilet." Betty, forty-three, Connie's youngest sister, said:

"Mother's still embarrassed because I do hair. I have had my own magazine, and I was art director for Flanders Filters for seven years. When I told my parents I wanted to do hair, they got me an apartment and a psychiatrist. He talked with me and said I was fine. I rent my own hair booth and work when I want to. I won't do what anybody tells me."—Bet took Germaine (a child from one of her classes) to get a shampoo today. "He didn't understand how to use it." I'll send Connie's Ode for her fiftieth from Durham. Fran says Teri Boone's contributed enough money for Edgar to play golf in the tournament with Perry Como at Duke.

To Connie, Jim's *gem*
Who knows kith and kin
in every con-ti-nent
Who paddles her boat
to our cottage for a float

We can see in July
she and Christopher riding high

We send our tri-butes
With whom we've shared many hoots.

Here's to many more, Connie
Your gift of spirit we enjoy!

Our love, Robin and Zoph

January 16, 1989—"eighty-five percent of the world's scientists whoever lived are living today."

Dear Colonel and Madame Berthier,

I think of you so often. I imagine that your beautiful house with Virginia Creeper was filled with family during Christmas. Are you going to the mountains this winter? Zoph and I are going to Florida the last week in March to see the Florida Keys and then to attend a conference of the board of directors of the Association of Broadcasters of North Carolina. We are delighted to be taking this trip.

Can you play tennis through the winter? Your daughter in England is very fortunate to have you so near. How are the grandchildren adapting? They have Paris for visits. Maybe Beatrice will come in this direction this summer. I hope so. Is this the year for you to travel? I hope so. We think that you could have a good time at our cottage beside the river.

My doctor says that I'm doing fine and that I have a lot of promise. Your letter is comforting because I appreciated deeply our unique and rare friendship and my memories of you and your charming family. Congratulations to Jean-Marc and Beatrice. I understand that they have succeeded in important exams.

My children say that I have a "punk" style now. Really, they want to give me a compliment. My hair fell out last June. But because of a chic wig, even strangers ask my advice on how to do their hair. My friends know better, but for the rest of the world, I just make up something. Friday I will have the help of gel to give me a style without the wig. When I begin chemo again in March, my hair will stay in!

Today is the birthday of Martin Luther King. Yesterday our minister mentioned that he was in Raleigh for a meeting that involved Blacks and Whites. On the steps of the capital were the Ku Klux Klan, full of hate. It's sad.

I love teaching: education will extinguish prejudice in time, I hope. In education one sees a lot of miracles all the time. Ryle has the opportunity to be an assistant in a pre-school. There is growing political support for school for three- and four-year-olds. I hope that the president will listen to Mr. Dukakis on this subject. They seem to agree.

Yesterday our neighbor, attending a private school near Washington, D.C., and a group of young visiting Russians, were invited to meet President Reagan.

I hope that the Reagans will keep their vitality in their retirement, like the Berthiers!

When a student called me last week for a French recipe, I thought of you, Madame. I gave her a short version of fruit tarts, thanks to the memory of your splendid apricot tart.

With deepest affection,
Robin

February 1989—Elizabeth, please tell Dr. Hadenmueller that I'm fine, but trying to finish some graduate work in the ECU English Department. Hopefully, I can get back to class in a few weeks.

February 19, 1989—Zoph and I raided friends' yards to fill our copper urns in memory of "The Potts Brothers"—Zoph and Fred—in church today. Jerry used a half-dozen situations to illustrate this point: "That, my friends, is what the kingdom is like—acting out the anti-structure even though we are still in the structure, doing the Father's will (Me: I have to whittle that down to what I believe I'm supposed to be doing here. I'm a deist. Except in emergencies) as though we were in heaven. And the funny thing is, when we do it, we already are." From: Sermon given by Jerry D. Bron, February 19, 1989. Title: "The Father's Will as the Kingdom." I believe that heaven is here if there is any to be found—and when. So this sermon shores me up.

March 27, 1989—A weekend with the Spoons and seeing their wine video. Spoon's wine cellar and wonderful chats. Their ambition and courage always stimulate me, with unique charm and humor. We've had a mutual admiration for thirty years.

March 29, 1989—Morgan, write this on the finest white stationery. Morgan, make a separate page for your extracurricular activities.

Dear Sir,

I am writing this letter to express my interest in attending the 1989 session of the Radio Broadcasting Camp. I am very interested in making radio broadcasting my career and I feel that your camp will help me learn more about radio broadcasting and how it works. I am familiar with how radio works because my father and grandfather have been working at a radio station for quite a while. I have been working at a radio station for quite a while. I have been going to the radio station to learn. My extracurricular activities are soccer, golf, radio, basketball, football, time with friends; also, Church Youth Fellowship, member of the cast of *The Music Man* in the high school production this spring, water-skiing, sailing, travel (Alaska, France, England, Switzerland), and dramas in the local Arts Council productions, and part-time work at the radio station WRRF—AM for President Zoph Potts, P.O. Box 1707.

Sincerely,
Morgan Potts

March 30, 1989—I walked through the cemetery around Thea Street to the lab. The wind was blowing, so I took off my earrings. In the hospital I put the earrings back on because the lab girls appreciate color. In lab today the nurse: "I'm really down. My first three patients really got me down. I hate what they have to go through. Mya Rouse, a good friend, had her breast removed last week. That's kinda close to home. She's doing fine. But who I pray for is her husband. He just lost a sister with cancer. But you. You're always so cheery—in such a good mood. You help me. Keep it up."

I didn't know she was aware of the big picture. I didn't know she is emotionally pulling for us. Upstairs in Dr. Raab's waiting room, a Mrs. Jackson says she remembers "Miss Sue's cookies. All the neighbourhood children used to go over for Miss Sue's sugar cookies. I used to work for them too, Miss Sue and Mr. Joe, for fifty cents a day. I would buy dress material for ten cents." My counts are lower than last week. "Stay out of crowds and away from people with colds. You must have chemo next Thursday, every twenty-eight days, if your counts are up, and they should be. There could be dividing, growing cancer cells, which we would miss the opportunity of zapping if we let you skip (delay) a week to go the Duke Hall of Fame Weekend. Of course, you can refuse."

"No. I do have good sense." The nurse called a lady from Robersonville. "Can you get here? We have your chemo. I understand. . . . I'm sorry it makes you sick. But you need it. Can we send someone to pick you up? You need twenty-four hours notice for a friend to bring you, so you can't come? Well, give me directions to your house and we'll come for you. You don't know roads, so you can't tell us?"

A lady taking chemo: "She don't have much of a friend. My friends aren't like that. She just don't want to come."

If I start medication two days before chemo, that means Tuesday, April 4, and I'll be doing the Cancer Crusade Banquet. The nurse: "There's one lady on chemo like you who called in to say that she was too tired to get out of bed. She goes to Durham and Charlotte starting up businesses. She's afraid to cut back. She could delegate, but she's afraid that if she does, that would be giving in. Then there's another lady on chemo who's the opposite. She says if the dishes don't get done, they'll wait—if she's tired."

March 31, 1989—Today in the *News and Observer,* Bill Morrison says that the advertising was artful and enchanting during the Emmy awards until GE broke the spell with a call for mammograms. Mary Sue gave me a chic haircut!

April 1, 1989—Hannah will play at the nursing home for me. Maybe I can rest up and get my counts up. She kicks up if she sees my picture or name in the paper, or doing for the Tuesday Cancer Crusade Banquet. I tell her that I really won't be there but ten minutes to do my part—need to avoid crowds right now. I do look green. Zoph says I looked different before during the first protocol too—the skin looks different. Hannah's cleared her calendar to play for me. Reed is in the air, due to Raleigh-Durham 8:00. Hannah says Linda is an inspiration to her Bible Study group and is especially close to Boogie. I tell her Linda's always helping me forward, but her Barney Seigel books depress me. Hannah says: "Rosebud said Mary Pete will be disappointed because I can't speak in tongues." Hannah told Rosebud: "Mother, you have your own special faith that you live. Mary Pete has suddenly discovered a faith and speaking in tongues. I've been once in a group where my hair stood on end. All I had to do was leave. They were speaking in tongues."

12:30—Teri Bergevin: "I know why the Cancer Crusade asked you to speak, because you tell it like it is. You're so positive." I like to be around people who gloss over it. They make me feel better. But I can't do that.

March—Foreign Language Collaborative—Source of pride: Coloring. Map colors—parts of body. Take home to use as a place mat. Tell me which site you are studying. Baby-doll clothes on a clothesline in classroom. Video fashion show narrated. Act when the teacher becomes angry.

Robin and Zoph. Duke Gardens. 1989.

Morgan. 1989.

Mother. May 25, 1989. 49th wedding anniversary.

Reed and Zoph. 1989.

Morgan, Mother, Ryle. 1989.

Existence of French in our town. Students bring anything with a French influence (examples lean cuisine). Hangings. Twister—put right foot in the Alps. Dolls Napoleon. They became interested in art. They realize art is very much a part of their lives. Renoir: going to ballet class. Visit from a dancing teacher. Jacques Cousteau. . . .

April 7, 1989—I'm achy. My shoulder is painful. My counts are low, so I'm bound to feel low. I'm focusing. Trying not to fold and cry and feel sorry for myself. But I'm always something wonderful to Zoph. Always.

Durham. Site of Duke's Washington Duke Hotel. Zoph worked on this land when he was seventeen and every summer during college. Now we're here in the elegant Washington Duke Inn and Golf Club to see Art Gregory inducted into the Duke Football Hall of Fame.

Zoph: "Your mother called to check on you. She wanted to know if she could give you some blood when I told her about your counts."

Robin: "It's harder on her. It's harder on you than me. I know from when you were sick. Thank God it's not my child."

Sitting by the fire, Art: "It's through Divine Intervention that I came here. I wanted to go to the Naval Academy, but the special afternoon English exam prohibited that. They don't require that anymore. The Citadel turned me down too. The Clemson coach called the Duke coach: 'Art really is not worth a shit, is he?' He was seeking confirmation of his decision not to give me a scholarship. I wanted to go to the Naval Academy for many reasons—one being that money doesn't matter—you're all in uniforms, taking the same courses."

Johnny Gregory, his brother, also an attorney, said: "Ed Howard (former Clemson coach just turned eighty, Alice McLure's dad) told a racial joke to a thousand people with black waiters everywhere." Nobody laughed. Then he said, "I know why you all didn't laugh. And if you don't start laughing, I'll tell it again."

Zoph: "Art always tried. Other people had as much talent but didn't try. That's why Coach Murray liked me. I was always trying. I knew he liked me. One time I heard him tell a player: 'You're the worst football player I've ever seen!' "

Zoph: "I'm not sure he could do any better."

Me: "Would Mr. Murray have said that if he knew Johnny couldn't do any better?"

Zoph: "Probably."

Me: "What kept you trying?

Zoph: "I've always been very positive. I'm always learning, always observing."

At the Duke Hall of Fame Induction: Even Dr. Bassett had to do sprints for being late for Coach Murray. Tom Butters—"greatest speaker at Duke, from the heart."

Dr. Frank Bassett, the team doctor since the '50s, and his wife, Miriam, at their After-the-Party party. Miriam gives us a tour of the house. A Scotsman designed it and the Duke Chapel. She passes Dr. Bassett's portrait; "He looks like Burt Reynolds to me." Later I mention this compliment to smiling Dr. Bassett: "I didn't know she thought I looked like Burt Reynolds. Did she say that? (Pause . . . looking pleased . . . reflection, then, laughter)" Miriam is very slender, about five feet six inches, very fair skin, chiseled small features, coal-colored hair, vermilion lipstick, straight-skirted bright print suit, just above the knees, three-inch heels. She must be about sixty-three, according to their long stint at Duke. She keeps saying, "I'm so glad you came." She says, "I only drink white wine and champagne."

Dr. Bassett remembers all the football maneuvers since. He is exuberant, reliving exciting sports and human events he's seen, Zoph's seen, and all who were at the party had shared. I, being so spacey, especially about football, had thought I'd feel left out, but I enjoyed every minute because they were all so excited to be together and shared a lot of laughs I understood. Miriam's five-year-old grandson took a treasured autographed football out in the rain. "He's the apple of my eye." Dr. Bassett didn't appreciate his treasure fading. He comes from Kentucky—a prestigious political and medical family (Miriam mentions). The Athletic Department's secretary, Mary: "Whenever recruits come to see the Bassetts, they always sign."

Miriam to me: "You drink like a Puritan. You don't look Puritan, but you drink like a Puritan." T. Moreman's fiancée received her engagement ring on the top of a Utah mountain. It was two sizes too big. They were afraid she'd lose it before she could ski down. Their wedding is October 14 in Duke Chapel. Mary, the secretary, dates T. Jr.'s father when he's in Durham. The fiancée says: "Mary can talk to the wall." Mary's face is very beautiful—she weighs about 240, is about 5 feet 3 inches. It's April so she says it's time for hose to go and she stays barefooted most of the party. It's forty degrees outside.

Dr. Leonard Baker. He's in his eighties. I mentioned seeing him dripping in from the ocean in March. He says, "Cold water never hurt anybody."—Young Connie. Her father is being inducted. She flies for Delta on the weekends, works with her husband in a T-shirt business during the week.

Leo Hart with George Thompson. Leo's father died when he was in the tenth grade.

"Coach Thompson is a father figure," says Zoph.

Dick Herbert: "The country's greatest sports writer." Nancy Rand: "Art has become proud of his heritage. Has a picture of the boat his father came over from Greece on at fourteen. He changed his name because his Greek one embarrassed him."

Sophie Gregory: "He's learning Greek now. He sent me a Christmas card in perfect Greek. He's doing very well. He went to Greece and didn't understand a word, so he decided to begin learning. I think it's good to learn other languages." Dan Hill: "Ace Parker was not the most reticent about his accomplishments—105 yard run. . . . He didn't want me to veer his thoughts away to my block. I kept asking him, 'Do you remember who I blocked?' Finally he said, 'No.' I told him I'd blocked our own teammate." Art's acceptance speech: "I'm most grateful to my father who emigrated to this country from Greece at the age of fourteen."

April 8, 1989—Saturday. My curiosity is what I'm honing. My mind could start growing. My mind intact could expand. Anything would be an improvement. If I look like I'd rather not, I can still be vital, still full of life, still an enabler. I can dress like mad too—Bobby Wyatt died this week at about fifty. Zoph's forty-eight and says: "It's an amazing story. After spring practice about 1960 at Duke football, Bobby was driving and ran off the road. He got mad and chased the car, lost control and wrecked . . . broke his back, paralyzed from the waist down. He went on, Master's, Ph.D. in Engineering. No family but a brother in Montana."—Frances Thompson's twenty-six, boyfriend wants to marry her. She is paralyzed from the waist down from an accident two weeks ago. Ryle teaches her son, who is beautiful like Frances.

I'm so ecstatic. When Zoph comes homes, he knows I'm very up. I tell him I have another project going: I do. I just called Bryan about doing a cover for my journal and I am thrilled about my "work," but I don't tell him that the pressure is off about chemo because he didn't (maybe) know I was particularly scared. He and I will never take another day for granted, but I do try to tell him just major spooks: I don't see how he handles my major fears as we both combat them together. I haven't done a thing on my own. I told Zoph tonight that Linda called to give me a pep talk. Zoph: "She's good about that, isn't she?" Robin: "I don't know how she does it. When I'm all through with this, I don't ever want to be around sick people!" (That's the old me talking.) The reason I write about cancer and me is so I can be of use if needed later. I want to be able to share, like Linda does for me. For example: "Get a wig immediately. Your hair's going in ten days!—and—You're doing great!" You're a fighter. You're like me. And it's been seven years and I'm counting on enjoying my grandchildren, just like you will be. You're doing great. I mean that."

April 10, 1989—Monday. A.M. I'm low today because I'm afraid I'm going on a spiral downward. My counts were too low to have chemo. What if they are still too low this Thursday? I'll just wither away with cancer. Linda calls. "How did you get along with your treatment? I thought about you." I tell her I couldn't have it and am on antibiotics. "Well, you're doing just like I did. Great. That chemo is working so well, killing all those cells—admittedly good cells—but it's working."

Robin: "But the nurse had said, 'No, you can't dare skip a week to go to Duke because there could be cancer cells forming and you must have chemo to stop them.' But then when she reads my counts, she says I can't have chemo and need an antibiotic."

Linda: "That's the pattern with chemo. At first your count stays the same (or lower somewhat) the first week: then, the second week, when you get to feeling better, you start feeling weaker because the chemo becomes in your system to the extent of killing cells."

Robin: "I never understood that—P.M. 3:30 Playing

George Gershwin, Jerome Kern for the folks and Rose-bud—she says "Pick it up a little." Ann Gayle sings along. Afterwards I walk across the lobby to check on Ella—There's Ann in her wheelchair singing "S'Wonderful. S'Wonderful."—I call Greenville to check on when they want my labs: "About 9:30 Thursday and then chemo." Hallelujah! I'm in the running again! She didn't say "If your labs are right." She said, *You will* have chemo!" Hallelujah!

April 1990—It's spring again. I've won! I'm living thanks to a new miracle drug. Who invented it? I should know. I should write to him or her and thank him or her; in Dr. Jo Allen's graduate course, Classics in Science, there's the opportunity. When I write to the company producing the drug, soon to arrive are the latest statistics on survival: there is only one woman still living in the U.S. in my category of disease. I start shaking with fear. How can I give a speech on this? Zoph listens to me rehearse and says that I can't end it like that. I search for hope: it's that I'm in first generation of survivors—we're making new stats!

1990s—When a famous model shows photos of her mastectomy to the Associated Press. I feel stunned for her and myself. Because Zoph has always assured me that to him I'm beautiful regardless, I'd never squared with my real looks. After seeing the mastectomy in the media, I continued to feel unsettled and unaccepting.

Spring 1997—At a dinner party when a friend locks into a favorite subject, bosom beauty, I feel furious. Zoph hears out my ranting: "I'm not bitter, but . . . " The next morning I knew I have the problem, not my beauty-extolling friend.

May 1997—Maybe I do have an option. Fear of not detecting reoccurring cancer stymies, and has so for ten years, my thinking. All doctors now say reconstructive surgery is appropriate, that after ten years it won't come back. I press—but what if? The doctors: It could still be found. Go forward.

June 1997—Morgan Alexandra, one year old, and I are dancing when she reaches in my bra and pulls out my stuffing. I laugh, but realize I do have a choice—that life is too short for me to waste any of it feeling bitter. . . . So the reconstruction's set for July 1, 1997. Zoph is calling it a closure. I feel deepening gratitude for life's serendipities—especially a friend waxing exuberance and a jigging granddaughter.

July 6, 1997—My breast reconstruction is more than I could have imagined. Not only do I have a magnificent (to me) new bosom, but stomach stretch marks from babies are masquerading now as the new bosom. Zoph thinks the effect is amazing. In a few months, we'll be off to a tenth-century basilica in Lyon, France, to celebrate a friend's marriage, and especially our own.

Morgan. Duke Soccer. Summer. 1989.

Charles. 1989.

Robin and Zoph. 1989.

Robin. 1989.

Robin and Christie. 1989.

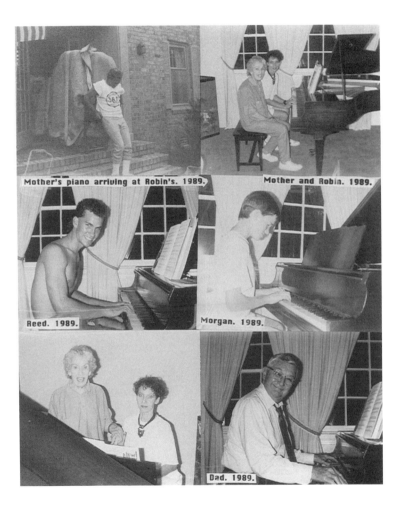

Mother's piano arriving at Robin's. 1989.

Mother and Robin. 1989.

Reed. 1989.

Morgan. 1989.

Dad. 1989.

FRAN
1989

Morgan and Zoph. 1989.

Mother and Ryle. 1989.

Robin. 1989.

Ryle. 1989.

Zoph. 1989.

Robin 1989.

Granny and Lilly. 1989.

Reed's 18th birthday. August 20, 1989.

Robin and Morgan. Summer.

Robin. Ocracoke Ferry. 27th Wedding Anniver

Mother

and Robin. Summer. 1989.

Reed and Robin. 1

Ryle, Coast Guard friend of Charles. Bryan. 1989.

Ryle. Halloween. 1989.

Charles' 23rd birthday. November 17, 1989.

Charles and Morgan. 1989.

Charles and Morgan. 1989.

Ryle and Pepper. November 17, 1989.

Zoph and Granny. Thanksgiving. 1989.

Granny, Robin, Mother. Thanksgiving. 1989.

Zoph and Granny. Thanksgiving. 1989.

Morgan. Fall. 1989.

Reed and Zoph, measuring. Fall. 1989.

Reed, Morgan, Ryle, Charles, Robin, Zoph. Fall. 1989.

Kay and Ryle. Noël. 1989.

Mary Ann. Noël. 1989.

Zoph and Robin. Noël. 1989.

Zoph, Granny, Kay. Noël. 1989.

Lilly and Dad. Noël. 1989.

Ryle, Zoph, Kay. Noël. 1989.

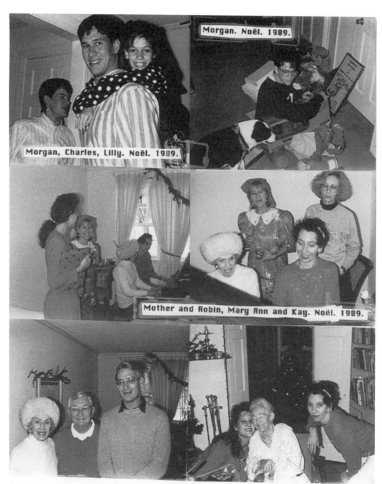

Morgan, Charles, Lilly. Noël. 1989.

Morgan. Noël. 1989.

Mother and Robin, Mary Ann and Kay. Noël. 1989.

Mother, Dad, Riley. Noël. 1989.

Ryle. Granny. Robin. Noël.

Christie and Robin. Noël. 1989.

Robin and Rosebud. Noël. 1989.

Zoph and Kay. Noël. 1989.

Ryle and Zoph. 27th birthday. February 27, 1990.

Morgan. Spring. 1990.

Ryle. February 27th, 1990.

Coastguardsman Charles in Coinjock. 1990.

Nook. Reed, from _Grease_. 1990.

Robin and Ryle. Coral Bay Club. Celebrating Mother and Dad's 50th anniversary. May 25, 1990.

Mother and Charles in Coinjock. 1990.

Charles. Coinjock. 1990.

Breakthroughs in Medicine
Classics in Science: Graduate school speech
Presented April for Dr. Jo Allen
and class, ECU

(Speech given by Robin Morgan Roberson Potts for the 1990 ECU graduate class of Dr. Jo Annen, "Classics in Science.")

Breakthroughs in Medicine

Until this assignment I didn't absorb the science about my status as part of a scientific experiment. There was no time for my research. I trusted my doctor and tried to exercise and rest and enjoy my well times. I knew I was taking part, but I'd never read what it was about. So with this assignment, I wanted to find out who to thank for the discovery of "my" drug that I'm counting on to save me.

Calvin Coolidge, Jr., son of the thirtieth president of the United States, died of blood poisoning on July 7, 1924. A week before, he had developed what appeared to be a trivial blister on his right great toe while playing tennis. Two days later he noted a sharp pain in the groin. Soon the correct diagnosis was established—septicemia, or invasion of the bloodstream by bacteria. An emergency operation was performed to establish drainage. All of the medical expertise of the country was brought to bear on the problem, but nothing could stem the relentless progress of the disease.

Twelve years later the phone rang in Dr. Perrin Long's laboratory. Dr. Long had for the past few months been engaged in clinical studies with the new drug sulfanilamide and was receiving calls from all over the country asking for advice about the use of the drug. He was also receiving a full quota of good-natured ribbing from his colleagues, who would call, announce themselves as some famous individual, and then give Dr. Long a dramatic but fictitious story about their problem. When he answered the phone that evening, he laughed and said, "You can't fool me this time. I know you are Eleanor Roosevelt." Then he abruptly hung up the phone. Within a few seconds, it rang again. This time he meekly said, "Yes, Mrs. Roosevelt, this is Dr. Long." The next day the newspaper headlines announced dramatically that the son of another president was ill, Franklin D. Roosevelt, Jr.; again, with blood stream invasion by streptococci. But this time the result was quite different, and later headlines signaled the news that the president's son had been cured by sulfanilamide. The beginning of a new era of "miracle drugs" was at hand.

In 1910, when Paul Ehrlich announced the discovery of salvarsan and its value in the treatment of syphilis, many believed that the control of infectious diseases was within medicine's grasp. Ehrlich coined the word "chemotherapy," meaning chemicals used in the treatment of disease. Ehrlich's goal was the destruction of the specific disease-producing living agents within the body of the patient—that is, the synthesis of chemicals whose target would be the invading organisms, killing them without any harm to the tissues of the patient.

Shortly after Ehrlich's world-shaking discovery, World War I began, and little more was done to advance research in this direction between 1914 and 1920. After the war, some important advances were made in the chemotherapy of tropical diseases, as evidenced by the development of atabrin for the treatment of malaria and tryparsamide for the cure of African sleeping sickness. In 1932, a new group of chemical agents called the "sulfonamide compounds" were tested for their effects upon streptococcal infections in mice. Successful results were first reported by Gerhard Domagk of Germany in 1935. The next six years witnessed a miraculous advance in the treatment of infectious diseases. The death rate from pneumonia was more than halved. Streptococcal bacteremia and meningitis, which had been almost universally fatal, were almost uniformly cured, and gonorrhea responded rapidly to the administration of sulfonamide drugs.

After World War II, a number of institutions became identified as clinical chemotherapy centers. A wide variety of agents were soon under study. The early studies provided the basis for the development of major advances in cancer chemotherapy. In 1965 the National Cancer Institute instituted a program for drug development. This program screened 15,000 new chemicals and natural products each year. The most promising compounds were studied clinically by a national network of physicians working in cooperative groups funded by National Cancer Institute grants. Important clinical gains have been possible because of the intensive use of cancer chemotherapy by such highly trained teams.

After World War II, massive financial support for medical research came from the federal government. The atomic bomb had been developed by unlimited funding of nuclear research, and the belief became prevalent that in order to conquer the remaining great killer diseases, such as cancer, cardiovascular disease, and kidney disease, it was necessary only to allocate huge sums to medical research. So much emphasis and so much money were devoted to research that medical education and medical care were relatively neglected at a time when both of these were increasingly almost prohibitive in cost. New forms of therapy. But as this twentieth century is ending, the major killer diseases are still unconquered.

Medical science advances in "explosion phenomena": the quiet build-up of bacteriology, which reached a critical level at about 1880, followed by the explosive discovery of the bacterial causes of many diseases within the span of little more than a decade; the gradual growth of knowledge about nutrition, reaching a critical level at about 1910, followed by the explosive discovery of vitamins. After World War II a number of unusually violent explosions occurred almost simultaneously, sulfur, penicillin, antibiotics.

Chemotherapeutic drugs are designed to interfere with the ability of the cancer cell to divide, grow, and perform its functions. There are many cancer types. Unfortunately, one of the most striking characteristics of cancer cells is their ability to adapt to toxic chemotherapeutic drugs, so that if the cells are not killed in the initial course of treatment, they become resistant to a drug's effects and eventually the drug becomes totally inactive against the cancer cells, although it continues to be toxic to normal cells. Curiously normal cells never seem to become resistant to chemotherapy, and this fundamental biological difference has not been fully explained. The ability of cancer cells to acquire resistance is beginning to be explained in molecular terms, and as we progressively define the mechanisms by which this happens, we find new avenues for designing chemotherapy. The idea is actually to exploit the adaptability of cancer cells and have them commit suicide by the very property that has protected them. A number of chemicals have been designed for this purpose, and some ingenious approaches are in various stages of testing.

To prevent being killed, a resistant cancer cell can have a mechanism by which it selectively fails to pump the drug into the cell, and if the cell acquires this property of keeping the drug on the outside, there is no way in which the cell will be damaged or killed. Another means by which the cell can become resistant to a drug is to increase the number of critical enzyme molecules that have to be blocked in order to destroy the cell.

Scientists are working at a feverish pace to learn more about the initial biochemical events that stimulate cells to become cancerous. The oncogene story gives us exciting new insights into how carcinogens activate specific regions of DNA to initiate the process of transformation of normal cells into cancer. This research is at such a fundamental level that it is difficult to predict how the information can be exploited, but it is safe to say that it will be used for the prevention of cancer. It is the individual variations in patients that ultimately determine how much of a chemical can be given before the point of tolerance is reached. Certain experiments are successful in animals but cannot be reproduced in humans because of different enzyme systems of control mechanisms, or differences in the way in which the drugs are handled by human tissues. One such approach that is right at the interface between test-tube research and clinical application is the stem-cell assay technique. By this method cancer cells are removed from patients, cultured in flasks, and different drugs tested to see which are effective. A drug that is not able to kill cells in culture will not usually kill them in the patient—that part of the prediction is good. However, an effective drug in culture is not necessarily effective when given to the patient.

The complexities of clinical research are very

great—one cannot just try out drugs by testing them in patients and seeing what happens. Anything but a rigorous approach is potentially life-threatening to patients and also likely to miss vital information. The ethics of clinical investigation are constantly under scrutiny.

The human body of 155 pounds has 77,000 billion cells. Cancer cells grow night and day; normal cells don't. When patients develop recurrent breast cancer or present with metastatic cancer, there is little chance of curing them (1981), although multiple treatments offer excellent control of the disease and its symptoms, many times for years. Most investigators now accept the concept that from early in its inception, breast cancer is a systemic disease with blood-borne or lymphatic micrometasteses being the rule rather than the exception. We must deal with the mammoth challenge of a tumor burden of between one billion and one trillion cells. Another problem facing the oncologist is the *stem cell*. This is the cancer cell that must be completely eradicated in order to achieve cure. Perhaps only 1 in 100 or 1,000 cancer cells is a stem cell, but these have the capability of rapid growth and replication of the entire tumor unless they are completely eliminated. Recent lab techniques for the identification of these cells have shed considerable light on their nature and even more importantly on their sensitivity to chemotherapeutic agents. A treatment that eliminates all of the stem cells would be curative.

In advanced breast cancer, our current treatment programs only eliminate five to six logs of the tumor stem cell pool and two to four logs of visible tumor. This is inadequate to cure the patient, and the tumor eventually regrows regardless whether a partial or complete response is achieved. The clinical response we all measure probably underestimates the actual log kill of the stem-cell pool. The fact that even with complete remissions, breast cancer recurs in the majority of patients indicates that an occult residual stem-cell pool persists.

Two recent reports provide useful data. Decker and others reporting for the Mayo Clinic describe the experience of forty-nine patients with a complete remission. These patients represented eleven percent of 438 patients treated with a variety of chemotherapy programs. With long follow-up, they conclude that cure was rare and only a single patient had remained continuously free of disease. The M.D. Anderson group from the University of Texas reported on 116 complete responders who had been treated with Combination Chemotherapy containing Adriamycin. This number represented nineteen percent of 619 patients who initially received chemotherapy. A total of forty-nine remained in complete remission more than two years, while twenty-eight had relapsed a median of nineteen months after stopping chemotherapy. However, twenty-one patients remained in complete remission thirty-one to seventy-two months after treatment, suggesting the possibility of cure.

Although at present, cure of advanced breast cancer is unlikely, it does not appear to be impossible and perhaps five to ten percent of patients will experience prolonged disease-free survival after treatment is stopped (*Adriamycin Report,* 1981).

In 1955, only a small group of optimistic researchers believed that chemotherapy could achieve an important role in cancer treatment.

In the thirty-two years since that article was published, there have been significant advances in the field of chemotherapy. Twelve cancers can now be considered curable, even at advanced stages. The period at risk varies among different cancers. These twelve tumors account for only about ten percent of all cancers.

Because of the recent improvements in remission rates

and survival duration in the intermediate groups, however, there is reason to be optimistic about the future curability of additional types of cancer. Combination chemotherapy is now the standard, and the regimens are complex and cyclical.

The best chance for significant benefit is with the first attempt at therapy. Drugs should be used in the maximum. Lowering dosage reduction to minimize toxicity is itself the most toxic side effect of chemotherapy and results in killing patients with misguided kindness.

Adjuvant chemotherapy is now well established in breast cancer. It appears to have had less effect on long-term survival than originally hoped, but has somewhat increased the cure rates in premenopausal women with axillar lymph node metastases.

My drug combination is Cyclophosphamide, Adriamycin, Fluorourcil: The median survival time of ER-positive patients treated with CAF (Cyclophosphamide, Adriamycin, Fluorourcil) is twenty-nine months (submitted September 11, 1986). The findings should be considered "hypothesis forming" not "hypothesis testing."

Nearly 280 years were to elapse after the introduction of cinchona bark into Western medicine before the next totally new drug became available for the systemic treatment of human infection.

Paul Ehrlich is justifiably revered as the founder of the science of chemotherapy, a term that for almost 100 years has been used specifically to describe the administration of chemical drugs deliberately produced for the treatment of diseases due to microorganisms or parasites. Ehrlich's work during this period was of paramount importance. It began at a time when the German chemical industry had just entered a very expensive phase following the discovery in England of the original mauve aniline dye by the eighteen-year old William Perkin in 1857, and in 1869, his subsequent publication of a commercial process for producing artificial alizarin.

Stemming from his studies in the 1880s on the distribution of dyes in the animal body and their specific fixation to various tissues, by 1891 Ehrlich had shown that methylene blue possessed specific affinity for malarial parasites and was moderately useful in human therapy. Another protozoal infection, trypanosomiasis, stimulated the first major advances in chemotherapy. Initial observations were made in British India by Alfred Lingard in 1893 on the treatment of the trypanosomal disease of cattle and horses known as surra. He found that arsenious oxide produced a good early effect, but owing to toxicity could not be used for long enough to obtain a permanent cure. Ten years later, when Harold Wolferstan Thomas in Liverpool successfully cured experimental trypanosomiasis using the less toxic arsenical atoxyl, he also showed that the drug was safe for human use by injecting himself intravenously with large doses.

Robert Koch was encouraged by this work to use atoxyl in human sleeping sickness.

On whether to tell patients about experiments: In the U.S. it is very difficult to provide informed consent in a meaningful way. We would have to say that we saw a difference but do not believe it, and now we want to prove it by asking patients to consent to the new study.

I asked my doctors (really, Jennifer) why didn't I get radiation along with chemo, that I had read that would have given me an edge. She said that it wouldn't have, that it was used in localized tumors. I told Jennifer about the experiment from the 60s wherein one-half of the women were given placebos, and the other half, chemo; none were told. Jennifer to me: "Aren't you glad you weren't living in the 60s with breast cancer?"

The experiment I am in is comparing taking an Adriamycin combo with and without a break as compared to a standard combo of Cyclophosphamide, Methotrexate, and Fluorourcil. Risks and benefits of my combo: It has not been proven that any treatment increases the chances for a permanent cure; all the chemicals depress the function of the bone marrow and lower the white blood cell count and the platelet count. These conditions increase the susceptibility to bruising, bleeding, or infections, which occasionally may be serious; Adriamycin has been associated with damage to the heart muscle, resulting in congestive heart failure in some patients. In addition, the chemotherapy is available outside of this study by consulting with a private physician who treats cancer patients.

Adriamycin binds DNA and inhibits nucleic acid synthesis, rapidly penetrates cells, but does not enter the brain.

The discovery of adriamin was a breakthrough. It was discovered in the 1960s by scientists in bacteria that grows in the sand around the Adriatic Sea.

Scientists collect samples all over.

For example, Vincristine comes from the periwinkle plant.

Another new chemo drug comes from the mold on the Sea Cucumber, which comes from the Sea Urchin family.

When I think about how far scientists have come, and how hard they are working, and how well they know what the problem is, I know that cancer will be conquered; and I expect to be here to celebrate.